DEAR FEMALE FOUNDER

66 Letters of Advice
from Women Entrepreneurs Who
Have Made $1 Billion in Revenue

Edited by **Lu Li**

Published by Blooming Founders Publishing.

ISBN: 978-0-9956081-0-8 (paperback)

For enquiries and information on bulk purchases, please contact Blooming Founders Publishing at publishing@bloomingfounders.com.

For more information on Blooming Founders and its support for female entrepreneurs, please visit www.bloomingfounders.com or follow us on Twitter @bloomingfoundrs.

This book is dedicated to all aspiring and budding female founders.

And the men, who support them.

Advance Praise

I love every story in this book and can't wait to share it with my own daughter. I wish I had access to these stories when I was younger and I recommend it as a gift to give to every mother and teacher you know. I would not have discovered that being an entrepreneur was my calling if I hadn't been inspired by Dame Steve Shirley, whose story was a case study at the London School of Economics where I was studying for my Master's degree – thank God for that! Bravo to Professor Bradley who put it on our reading list and bravo to Lu Li for creating this book of stories which make compelling reading. I have no doubt it will change the world for the better. Stories worth sharing! Share them!

Sherry Coutu CBE

Dear Female Founder is a personal, inspirational and at times a deeply moving read. I wish it had existed when I started my own entrepreneurial journey – it would have saved me a lot of time and heartache! The range of experiences and advice make it an invaluable read for every aspiring entrepreneur – male or female!

Sarah Wood OBE

Anything that encourages more women to go out there be bold and start something gets a big tick from me.

Baroness Martha Lane Fox CBE

Dear Female Founder is an inspiring, candid and often touching anthology of lessons and stories from female entrepreneurs. I wish I had access to a resource like that when I set up my first business 15 years ago. I'd have certainly felt more confident to be myself and not been embarrassed to be vulnerable and ask for more support. Everyone should read it regardless of gender.

Wendy Tan White MBE

Dear Female Founder lets you learn from the experience, emotional ups and downs and the wisdom gained by those who have done it before you – rather than learning frameworks or rules like most business books. The stories make it real in a way no other book has.

Gil Penchin a

I wished this book had existed when I started my journey as an entrepreneur. Dear Female Founder is as inspiring as it is honest. A must read if you are thinking about taking the journey into the world of startup or want to inspire the next generation of female founders that they can do it too.

Kathryn Parsons

Dear Female Founder is no average "How to become a successful entrepreneur" read. It's a unique blend of encouragement, wisdom and practical insights, shared by remarkable female entrepreneurs. Whether you're a budding female entrepreneur or an intrapreneur within a bigger company, the rich advice will stand you in good stead and undoubtedly inspire you. It's also a well overdue celebration of the success stories of brilliant women from all over the world.

Paul Frampton

CONTENTS

Part 3   REFLECT

FOREWORD

When I started as an entrepreneur in the late 1980's, nobody even used that word. In fact, when I told my parents that after graduating from college, I wanted to work at a startup, they said "but what are you going to do for a living?" Being an entrepreneur back then was a bit like being an inventor - it was that thing your crazy uncle did as a hobby in his garage on the weekends. I like to joke that after graduating with a degree in computer science, my conservative friends went to work at IBM and my progressive friends went to work at Microsoft. Starting your own business just wasn't cool.

We've come a long way since then in making entrepreneurship more appealing to people of all ages. The problem, however, we still have a long way to go in making it appealing to people of all color and genders too. It's kind of crazy if you think about it, why would we want to exclude half of the talent pool as co-founders, employees and executives? In addition, our own research and research of many others has shown that diverse organizations have a higher likelihood of success. Why shouldn't we all give ourselves a leg up? This is a problem that time will fix, as we grow and learn. But we need role models to help guide us, just as I had to seek out people like me when I was getting started. We need to hear the stories of others to inspire us on our journey.

In these pages, you'll find these stories. Entrepreneurship continues to change and evolve for the better. I hope that you find these stories inspiring and that they help you on your journey.

David Brown,
Co-founder and Managing Partner, Techstars.

Boulder, CO
March 25, 2016

INTRODUCTION

"Life is not easy for any of us. But what of that? We must have perseverance and above all confidence in ourselves. We must believe that we are gifted for something and that this thing must be attained."

– Marie Curie

Dear Female Founder,

There is a new zeitgeist around women's empowerment, and we like it. Whether it's Beyoncé singing "Who runs this world?", Sheryl Sandberg asking women to 'lean in', Sophia Amoruso creating the #GIRLBOSS movement, or Cara Delevingne wearing T-shirts with 'THE FUTURE IS FEMALE' in bold capital letters, there are inspiring vibes all around, encouraging you to stand up for yourself, unapologetically.

At the same time, the narrative around professional success has changed and entrepreneurship is now widely accepted, or is even seen as a desirable alternative to traditional career paths. Mainstream media reports about how young entrepreneurs found riches with platforms and applications they have built in their dorm rooms. You start hearing more about the pitch competitions they win, the accelerator programmes they join, and the investment money they raise.

At the intersection of these developments, you – an ambitious, educated, talented female individual – are intrigued by the idea of living life on your own terms, doing something meaningful, and perhaps building a successful business empire along the way. Possibly you even have a great idea where you see a big market opportunity?

I have met hundreds of women who are in this state of mind. It's amazing to see their ideas, and it's also saddening to hear the thoughts that come after that. "I'm not sure, I am quite ready yet", "I don't have a lot of experience in business", "I don't know anyone else who is actually a successful entrepreneur. I don't have a mentor to help me with my business", and "The startup and business world favours white men and I don't fit into that category. I'm not sure whether I can do this".

If you can relate to any of these thoughts, then you will benefit hugely from this book. But before we get into details, you probably want to know who is writing to you, right? Here is why I created this book:

My name is Lu Li and once upon a time, I thought that climbing the corporate ladder in a prestigious company was the ultimate goal for my professional life. I was born in China and arrived in Berlin, Germany, at the age of 6. My parents were immigrants surviving on a small stipend that my dad received to do his PhD degree. Thanks to the permeability of the German education system (which also came largely for free), I was able to work my way into a very good university, got into a mentorship programme at McKinsey, and eventually started to work for 'The Firm' after graduation.

I put in long hours at every company I worked for, eager to learn and contribute. It was an amazing experience at first, but after a couple of years I witnessed change, which shook up the organisation. I was still giving a lot, but the company no longer loved me back. Suddenly, I felt uncertain about my career progression, I questioned whether my strengths were fitting the jobs on the next level and I was fed up with having to navigate corporate politics and working for someone else's agenda.

A little voice said to me "You can do much better on your own", and I knew it was time to leave. I jumped off the corporate ladder, determined to create my own future as an entrepreneur. After all, I have aced everything else in my life so far, so why not be successful being my own boss?

Today, I smile when I think about how naive I was at the time. Thankfully, entrepreneurship is an unforgiving teacher and I was brought back to earth quickly. After 3.5 years, starting and abandoning 2 businesses, I know for certain that it is *not at all* easy to build a sustainable business. Additionally, I found that there *are* differences between the journey of a female founder versus the one of a male founder.

I believe that there is a need to reinvent the experience of startup incubation to address the challenges that women face. I also believe that women are the most under-tapped resource for economic improvement, so I really wanted to succeed in helping other women succeed.

That's why I started building Blooming Founders, an organisation that helps to accelerate the startup journey of female founders, as my third business. We produce inspirational and educational events in London and we also run a kick-ass online community where experiences, advice and knowledge are exchanged. Every member is committed to help one another; we believe that 'a rising tide lifts all ships'. We are growing quickly and internationally, also supporting other communities that share our mission, and I cannot wait to see what amazing things all of us can do together.

Running this community gave me unique insights about female entrepreneurship in a broader context and the challenges that women encounter. One of the key things that hold women back is the lack of role models. I used to ask community members about the female founders they admire the most, but most of the times I was met with silence.

No one comes to mind, not in her respective field anyway. This is both startling and alarming. Why?

Let me echo Sheryl Sandberg, who we all know, Marian Wright Edelman, Founder and President of the Children's Defense Fund, and Sally Ride, the first American woman in space:

"You can't be what you can't see".

We need stories, examples and idols, which prove to us what is possible and who embody ways we want to mimic. There are thousands of trailblazing female founders in pretty much every industry and country. Yet we don't know about many (or any) of them – and that is the issue. If the future is really female, then we have to shine more light on those female role models, who are innovators, founders, investors, and advisors to founders, to encourage other women to follow their paths.

And this is the purpose of this book: to showcase a diverse spectrum of women, who have done and achieved amazing things in entrepreneurship. Some of them are still in their twenties, some of them have several children, some of them fell into entrepreneurship, and some of them were born that way. Many are based in startup hubs like Silicon Valley, New York, London or Berlin, but many operate from much less developed ecosystems like Argentina, Jordan, Indonesia, and New Zealand. I want you *see* that it is never too early or too late to become a founder, and that you can do it from anywhere in the world.

But that is not all. This book is also a concentrated resource uncovering startup advice and business wisdom from 66 women, who have in total raised over $85 million investment, generated over $1 billion in revenue and created over 2000 jobs. Each chapter comes in form of a letter that they have written to you, the next generation of female founders, sharing their first-hand insights on lessons learnt and things they wished someone had told them at the beginning of their startup journey.

I am excited to present to you the knowledge from over a hundred years of experience in business and entrepreneurship. While editing, it certainly felt like I was listening to 66 new mentors, making their learnings my own, and feeling incredibly uplifted by their words to continue my own entrepreneurial path.

Whatever your mind can conceive and believe, you can achieve. Look at Heather Russell, who moved to Japan without speaking Japanese and built a multi-million dollar business there. Or Nadezhda Robinson, who has a Russian name, is a woman of colour, and runs a business designed around lifestyle consumption of Chinese millennials. Or Danae Ringelmann, who changed the way ideas get funded across the world, democratising access to capital, in particular for women entrepreneurs.

Before we dive in, I would like to note that the content of this book is the outcome of a creative experiment (that's what we do as founders, we try new things!). My only ask from our contributing authors was for them to write about the things they deemed most impactful for the future generation, and as a result, I received a colourful range of thoughts and styles as diverse as the women who authored them. It was challenging to arrange them in order, but in the end, I have found three categories to group them into: letters that inspire you ("START"), letters where you can distract immediate learnings ("LEARN"), and letters that deserve some contemplation ("REFLECT").

As every letter stems from unique, personal experiences, it will be natural that some of them will resonate with you more, and some of them will resonate less. You might also notice some overlap in the advice that they share, which only emphasises the need to give those areas more consideration. Whether you read this book cover to cover, or in small doses, the most important thing for you to know is:

You are not alone.

Behind every contributor, there are many other fearless female founders, who are pilgrims of the same journey as yours, whether it is a high-growth tech startup, your own product line, a service-based SME, or a career as a self-employed freelancer. If you are just starting out, then these women can be the best mentors and advisors for you.

I cordially invite you to meet them in our community which you can join at www.bloomingfounders.com; some of the contributors are there too.

My hope for this book is that it will inspire you to face your doubts and (continue to) pursue your entrepreneurial dreams. Remember, the world needs your ideas, your unique set of skills, your leadership style, and your passion to become a better place. There are unlimited opportunities to be seized and unprecedented value to be created. The contributors of this book were not deterred by the challenges they faced, and we should not be either.

Keep blooming!
Lu

Part 1
START

"Every accomplishment starts with
the decision to try."

Letter No. 1

Alex Depledge, Co-Founder of Hassle.com

Dear Female Founder,

It's okay to not fit in. Yes, seriously.

I know that all the signals society gives us tell us that is not the case, but it is true.

In school, we want to run with the cool girls and adhere to the path laid out for us: ace your GCSE's, nail your A-Levels, get into the best university, land that coveted graduate scheme.

We want to be good in bed, but not known as easy. We shouldn't be too loud, but shouldn't be too quiet, either. We want to make your parents proud and have our teachers like us, but we don't want to be seen as their pets. Who invented all these norms? Not us, did we?

In fact, I discovered something when I hit thirty. After I had laboured under the weight of regret for years for saying the wrong thing, second-guessing my passion, and apologising for my style, I suddenly realised that *difference* is my (and your) greatest asset. I realised that all the coaching I had received around my personal brand, getting ahead, cutting through the noise all equated to difference.

By now, you are thinking, "Oh shut up, I have heard this all before". And it is true. I'm sure you will have, but how often have you paused and checked your behaviour?

We all say the lines, but we don't believe them. Don't lose twenty years like I did, knowing but not internalising. How many of you look back on younger photos and think "Damn, I looked good"? Yet, at the time you probably believed that you would have looked better if you had lost weight, had a different haircut or wore a better dress.

Female confidence is the single biggest inhibitor of progression. My mother told me as a teenager, that everyone in the room was pretending. It wasn't till a few years ago, that I recognised what she described as imposter syndrome. Any successful person I ask (male or female) admits to feeling this most of the time. See, we are all pretending.

We will not punch through that glass ceiling until we believe we can. Till we sleep with who we want to, as often as we like, pursue the activities that make us happy, love with abundance, trust our guts over data, pull the girl up behind you, love and appreciate the body we have been given and be unafraid to sit outside the norm.

Embrace your difference. It is your secret weapon.

I am sure you are thinking, "Great, but what tangible things can I do to build confidence, and maybe even become an entrepreneur?"

Here are a few:

1. Eat your frog everyday. Take the worst thing on your to-do list and do it first. It is amazing how productive the rest of the day will be, if we don't procrastinate on ugly tasks.

2. If you're scared before a meeting, pitch or anything, go to the bathroom, look in the mirror and say these words: "I am the shit". It does amazing things for confidence.

3. It's all about customers, no one else. Don't be arrogant and think you know what they want. Talk to them every day and hear it from them.

4. Starting a business is like painting or writing – you just have to start. Stop talking about your ideas and start doing something about them. *Anything* is good. Starting is the hardest thing, I know, but I'd be very proud of you if you'd start something today.

With love,
Alex

About the author:

Alex Depledge is the straight talking businesswoman behind British tech success story Hassle.com – one of the most acclaimed startups to emerge from London's Tech City. She co-founded the business in 2012 and raised $6 million in funding from Accel Partners in 2014. In 2015, Hassle was acquired by German rival Helpling for a reported €32 million. Included on the 2016 Debrett's 500 Most Influential People List and named as FDM Everywoman 'Startup Founder of the Year', Alex is currently chair of Coadec (Coalition for a Digital Economy) and a Venture Partner with Ignite 100, a prominent European based angel-led accelerator programme. She has also been awarded an MBE for services to the sharing economy by HRH Queen Elizabeth.

Letter No. 2

Gina Bianchini, Founder and CEO of Mightybell and Co-Founder of LeanIn.org

Dear Female Founder,

I often get asked about advice for young women who are looking to become entrepreneurs, and I would typically scope my answer to the Silicon Valley type of technology entrepreneurship, since this is what I know best.

Recently, I watched an interview with Lin-Manuel Miranda. He said something that stuck with me: "I picked a lane."

He was talking about going to a highly competitive high school in New York City. He knew that to excel in this environment, he had to focus on one thing (theater) and kick ass (creating not one but two Broadway-changing productions).

Fast-forward to 2016, and Silicon Valley has become the single most competitive professional environment on the planet. Where 20 or 30 years ago, the masters of the universe went to Wall Street to make their fortunes, today those same unapologetically ambitious people (primarily, but not exclusively, men) make their way to Silicon Valley.

For these 0.0001% of the most competitive humans on the planet, anything they can do to keep out additional competition (other founders, not employees, they want employees), they will do. It's human nature.

Then, these competitive founders become competitive venture capitalists, and they take the same ways they sized up the competition as operators into the ways that they evaluate founders, giving more credibility to those formidable foes they met in past battles going all the way back to the playground.

This is the arena.

It's not an arena that's easy for anyone. However, given this context you can see how technology entrepreneurship among competing masters of the universe is especially challenging for women and people of color to dive in.

I don't have to tell you this; the social science research and basic statistics do the work for me. But it also isn't the point. The only question an entrepreneur should ask is, "What do I need to do to win in the arena?"

Here are a few things I believe make it possible to compete effectively when you don't fit the dominant pattern of people who were born with every opportunity and the expectation that they could be the next Bill Gates:

Pick a lane. Don't just start a tech startup to start a tech startup. It's too hard. Rather, go deep on a mission, market or domain that captures your curiosity, and that you can imagine working on for the next 10 years. Get extraordinarily good at what you do. Be so good that people come to you for your expertise.

Put down the playbook. The startup playbook is fed by endless posts by newly minted venture capitalists about what they look for in entrepreneurs, what they think makes a great pitch, how you should talk about your market and what growth hacks work today. The audience for this playbook fits a certain profile of entrepreneur who will be judged on their potential more favorably than you will be as a woman or person of color. That's not meant to be a bummer. It's a fact.

As an entrepreneur, you figure out how to hack around facts.

Control your own destiny. Use shortcuts and as little capital as you can to start generating revenue. To hack around the facts, I believe the most important question to ask yourself is, "How do I get them to come to me?"

Adi Tatarko at Houzz created the company with her husband before taking a dollar of investment. She saw the opportunity to bring together the supply of professionals and home decorating enthusiasts that makes Houzz special. She and Alon created something people loved. Including investors. They came to her.

When I look at success stories like Houzz, or SurveyMonkey and GitHub, who both bootstrapped their way to revenue before raising money, they all figured out how to show massive growth and revenue without capital. It's possible.

This is a different playbook and I believe will be how women and people of color create massive, billion-dollar companies that need to exist in the world.

Work smarter, not harder. This is the most non-intuitive observation I will probably make. I work hard. I also mentor amazing entrepreneurs who happen to be women or were born a different color than me and work twice as hard for half the credit.

If you want to compete in the arena, hard work isn't enough. And judging yourself on how hard you work, rather than how smart you work can be fatal.

If you value hard work alone, you'll think it is an entrepreneur's job to slog out a 10-month fundraise to get a $250,000 or $500,000 check, when an entrepreneur who fits the pattern just raised $5,000,000 in a few weeks with a competitive process.

Your job as an entrepreneur in this situation is not to say, "I'm going to just keep going." It's to say, "What can I do to show results or build the thing I am passionate about bringing into this world without needing anyone's money?"

This is your chance to work smarter. You can find shortcuts that allow you to serve your market and show amazing results before you have to raise a dime.

It might mean a Kickstarter project, hacking together something yourself or with friends (but beware of bad MVPs), tapping a Mightybell Network to validate the opportunity for a new kind of network around a shared identity or interest, a MailChimp list to build the next TheSkimm with sponsors, or a Dwnld app to start a new media company.

If you work smarter, you'll win.

All my best,
Gina

About the author:

Gina Bianchini is an American entrepreneur and investor based in Silicon Valley. She is currently the founder and CEO of Mightybell, a software platform for people and companies to create their own communities. Before founding Mightybell, Gina led Ning, the largest social platform for communities, which she co-founded with Marc Andreessen in 2004. She has appeared on Charlie Rose, CNBC and CNN and serves on the board of directors of Scripps Networks Interactive. Gina is also the co-founder of Sheryl Sandberg's Leanin.org, where she crafted and launched Lean In Circles. She graduated from Stanford University in 1994 and has also been featured on the cover of Fortune magazine.

Letter No. 3

Alexandra Greenhill, Co-Founder and CEO of myBestHelper.com

Dear Female Founder,

There are so many reasons to avoid and delay starting the journey of building your company, some of them are practical and some of them you are barely aware of.

And yet, begin you must, because you know deep in your heart, or gut, or mind, wherever the wisdom resides, that this is something you just have to do. So don't delay the inevitable – just do it, and keep in mind that a journey of a thousand steps begins with just one. Declare your intent to the universe and embrace what happens next, even if it doesn't follow your expectations or the 'normal' rules of business life.

In practical terms, this means you need to describe in a great amount of detail the problem you are solving and for whom. Then and only then can you sketch out your idea of what is your product or service, which is likely to change many times before you succeed. Fall in love with your problem and your users; don't fall in love with your solution. This way you are sure to enjoy the journey and to increase your odds of success.

Speaking of which, you also need to define what success is for you. Be specific and don't just describe what you think is achievable. Dare to access your dreams and put onto paper what would be an amazing, hard-to-believe outcome of your venture. Don't make it bigger or smaller just because of what others say – make it into what would be a real dream come true for you. You have to aim for what you really want, if you want a real chance of getting it. It's heartbreaking to see founders achieve the success that others admire, but doesn't reflect what they really wanted.

Deciding to embark on the journey of starting your own business doesn't mean that you have to do it all alone, or that it will all be hardship. On the contrary, my advice to you is if the going is too hard, find an easier path or better yet, discover your posse – your crew, a group of people who will come along with you, give you advice and support, and show you shortcuts to the goals you have set.

Some of your supporters will be people close to you who have no idea what business you are in. They cheer you on and remind you of who you really are. Some are business experts, and their input is more relevant to the company you are building. Some you will never know in person, but you will read their wisdoms or see their videos outlining hard lessons learned. Lean on that goodwill, ask for and accept help when it's available to you.

It's equally important, in my opinion, to stop hanging out with whoever is slowing you down or being negative. It's tough enough to make it all happen, and you need your cheerleaders along, so don't tolerate any detractors on the journey – you'll go faster and it will be more fun. Choose your partners, investors and employees wisely. If they are not stellar human beings or they are not really passionate about your concept, no matter how much expertise, talent or money they represent, please take my advice and walk away.

Once you have your concept and team, there are practical matters to be handled: gathering resources, planning first steps, getting set up with permits and office. Lots of great advice is available nowadays, so use it.

Most importantly, find approaches that resonate with you and just follow those; trying to be something you are not, usually doesn't work and is not sustainable.

A fantastic shortcut is to build on brand names – adding team members and advisors who have worked for well-respected organizations, and/or have gone through competitions and accelerators that are well-known brands. Another great shortcut is to learn to appreciate people who quickly tell you 'no', and especially the ones who clarify why. They will help you grow the most and will also help you get faster to the ones who will say 'yes'.

Even with perfect conditions, shortcuts and all, keep in mind that even the fastest founders don't usually run a marathon at a sprinter's pace. You need to persist. Evolve your business until you get the feedback from customers that you have hit the right solution for their needs that is also the right concept to take you to your personal definition of success for the business. Both are key to making your company great and enduring.

My final and most important piece of advice to you: whatever you do, you should find your way of making this entrepreneurial journey a fun endeavor rather than a rollercoaster of terror.

Managing one's energy and personal life, not treating every setback as the end of the world, finding joy in the learning and doing are the three core skill sets of founders who thrive while making their idea a reality and building a kickass business.

How do I know all of this? Firsthand as a physician/mom-turned-tech entrepreneur, as well as from having seen so many others and learning from their successes and hardships. This is the advice I wish someone had given me when I started my company.

Now go and discover what you are capable of (with a little bit of help from your friends, of course!).

Alexandra

About the author:

Alexandra Greenhill is an award-winning Canadian physician leader and tech CEO. She is a mom of three and the co-founder and CEO of myBestHelper.com, a company that is reinventing how people are supported in daily life and times of need. myBestHelper has received many recognitions, including the Cartier Women's Initiative Award 2015. Alexandra believes that entrepreneurship is the answer to the greatest issues we face today and the journey to amazing accomplishments starts with being unreasonable enough to want to succeed at the 'impossible'.

Letter No. 4

Christina Richardson, Co-Founder of Openr

Dear Female Founder,

This is the hardest job I've ever had – and I love it.

Nothing prepares you for a life of entrepreneurship. I spent a decade managing multi-million pound budgets for some of the biggest food and drink brands in the world, but nothing compares to the fear of making payroll, or the exhilaration of making your first sale.

I was always going to be running my own company. Some would say the die was cast early. I was selling hand-made jewellery at age 14 and launched my first business at 19 years old – but I had a journey to go on, and so the next 10 years were all about learning everything I could from the corporate world to pave the journey.

For 5 years now, I've been in the thick of the entrepreneurial ecosystem – becoming known for entrepreneurial marketing (advising, mentoring, teaching) and launching two marketing technology companies. Typically I'm asked for marketing advice, but this is an opportunity to reflect more widely on the things that contribute to progress when doing it alone. Some I've had to learn, some I still battle with everyday. But they're worth the battle, because at the end of the day, this is the best job in the world.

No more talk on risk

Through the first half of my career I was convinced I was risk averse, yet given I've spent years without a dependable salary (with a mortgage to pay) that notion is laughable. The truth is, entrepreneurs are not frivolous risk takers, they are calculated decision-makers.

Find the thing that you feel is a calculated good bet and try it. For me (and for many I've since mentored) that has been working out what you need to live on, and then working out how your venture could cover that. This is often fewer sales than you think, and it's a much more achievable goal to get there. Break everything down to its constituent parts and the roadmap feels much more achievable.

Start fast, fail faster

The second key ingredient to a calculated entrepreneurial leap is proof; yet so many want to spend big and launch big, which is the high road to failing big. Launch the very smallest version of your idea (ideally just a sign-up page) and get it in front of real people.

As the army mantra goes, 'no plan survives the first encounter' and the truth is, no matter what you thought you should launch, it will not be what real customers actually want. So find out early and iterate from there. This applies to every element of business beyond (especially marketing activities) – try it, test it, iterate and repeat.

If something scares you, learn how to do it

Type A's aren't all that comfortable saying they don't know something. Well, get comfortable. There is no such thing as only doing 'the nice bits' when you're launching your own business, so get ready for a steep learning curve.

I'm a firm believer in never asking someone to do something you don't have a basic understanding of yourself. Learn how something works and the fear of not knowing (and of trusting another) disappears. So research, learn and crack on.

Open up to a world of help

Everyone says networking is key but I think we all go on a personal journey to discover just how true it is. My journey started when I was still in my corporate security blanket, but planning my next steps. I decided to reach out to everyone I knew whilst trying to quash concerns that they wouldn't remember me, or wouldn't have time to help.

I tentatively wrote a 'cold' email to someone I had not seen in 8 years (!). That person, not only remembered me, but also took me out for dinner with bucket-loads of enthusiasm to impart her wisdom, and repeatedly told me I should absolutely 'do it'. Every person I met had some advice, and the truth is that everyone loves to feel knowledgeable. So ask away and don't forget to ask, "Is there anyone you know that you think I should speak to?"

Ask, ask, (did I say ask?)

This is one I still strive to master everyday (I talk too much) but it's worth the effort. Start every meeting with the 3-question mantra in mind. Ask 3 questions of customers, investors, influencers and each and every encounter will uncover valuable insight that will help you build a business that truly resonates with buyers. Your core aim is to build a tribe who LOVE what you do. Always asking 'why' means you're focused on understanding them, and can deliver the product they need in a context relevant to them.

Craft a story and share it far and wide

Your most important job as founder is to mobilize people behind you, because a one-woman mission just won't cut it. Create a vision of the future that motivates; craft a story behind how you got here and why you're on this mission; then use it to on-board others to the mission. Having a vision of what you want to achieve, and where you want to get to, is infectiously compelling – to your consumers, to your team, to any potential investors. Be proud of yours and use it.

Invest in people like others invest in you

I am grateful everyday to those that spent time training and mentoring me, and I believe fervently that we should all do more than our bit to pass on support. If you invest time in every new starter, the simple economics show that they'll deliver better, quicker. Continue to invest in their training and they'll continue to get better and stay with you longer. You need great people for your team, so help make them great and revel in helping another person on their journey too.

Read something inspirational every week

Once you're up and running you will be sucked into the every-day; yet achieving that mission means thinking bigger, reflecting and planning ahead. I was slow to learn this one, but discovered that putting aside an hour every week to read a business-related book was just the inspiration I needed to do this.

Happiness is defined by you – celebrate every day

Entrepreneurship is about mental toughness: it's not those that get funding, or have more contacts, or have better ideas that actually succeed (though all these things are helpful). It is those who control and overcome the mental challenges like fear and doubt that make it. Things will always go wrong, and it is your reaction that defines you. So at the end of each day, find three things that went well and have a little mini-celebration. Seeking out the positives make the tough bits surmountable.

Be bold, be brave and try it.

Christina

About the author:

Christina Richardson is a British entrepreneur and the co-founder of Openr, a marketing-tech platform, used by global brands and SMEs alike, to drive action from all the content that they share online. Christina spent much of her career managing and growing FMCG brands at Nestle and Robinsons, then turned her hand to young start-up brands, and has never looked back since. She also teaches Entrepreneurial Marketing for University College London (UCL), and is a mentor at UCL and Bathtub2Boardroom. She is a regular speaker at industry events including those at The British Library and writes regularly for industry publications like Marketing Donut, as well as the business publications of HSBC, BT and Vodafone.

Letter No. 5

Nisa Amoils, Investor at New York Angels

Dear Female Founder,

2015 was a banner year for you and it is going to get even better!

There are an unprecedented number of resources available now, there are more women angel investors looking to fund your earliest raises, and some great women VC's looking to invest in the next phase of growth (and hopefully more). That is because there are women entrepreneurs who have paved the way and proven that they *can* have big valuations and exits. Financial return speaks its own language.

While women still receive less institutional funding than men, there are increasingly more savvy investors who realize that this is an arbitrage opportunity. There are more funds being established that specifically invest in women. A well-known VC in New York even released a report indicating that female-led companies outperformed their male counterparts. Investors are listening.

Pick a large problem that you are passionate about solving and that you are uniquely qualified to solve. Timing is everything. Ask yourself: What factors have changed in the marketplace to make it the right time for this business to thrive? Demographic shifts? Technological advances? Change in needs?

Know why each investor is right for your business and approach them. Do your research to see what types of companies he or she likes to invest in. Try to talk with other portfolio companies to get references on style. The investor should be passionate about your business.

Be prepared when pitching to investors and know your numbers. In consumer businesses, it is all about customer acquisition cost and marketing plan relative to the lifetime value of a customer. On the enterprise side, it is the rate at which you can close sales and scale. At the seed stage of investment, projections are good to have, but be aware that they may not turn out to be accurate as the business grows or changes. Stay on top of your numbers as the business evolves.

Pick a great advisory board and use them to have regular information updates or meetings. If you don't have connections in your industry, you can find and reach most people on social media. It doesn't have to be someone you know, but be aware that they might want some equity in return to join your board. Also, don't be afraid to share bad news with your investors and board; transparency and honesty trumps everything.

Entrepreneurship is challenging and you will need a good support system. Don't do it by yourself – many investors see single founders as a risk factor. You can start by yourself, but spend a lot of time looking for a co-founder who has complementary skills to yours.

Whatever you do, don't be apologetic about it and try to avoid saying "Sorry" when it's not necessary.

Go ahead and explore new fields and nontraditional paths – you may find more of a meritocracy there. For example, 38% of the entrepreneurs in the Cannabis industry are female and I believe that we will see more women leaders emerge over the next few years in those untapped industries.

I would love to see more female founders in areas of frontier technology such as robotics, drones, autonomous vehicles, remote sensing, machine learning and artificial intelligence, augmented and virtual reality, and cyber security. As an investor in these areas, I see too few women and the time is right for these businesses to thrive.

Be bold and chase your dreams!

All my best,
Nisa

About the author:

Nisa Amoils is an active early stage investor, Board advisor and entrepreneur. She is a member of New York Angels where she invests in a variety of technology and is the co-chair of the frontier technology committee which encompasses AR/VR, robotics, drones, AI, driverless cars, autonomous innovations, cyber security, remote sensing, blockchain and other disruptive technologies. She is a regular judge/panelist on CNBC, MSNBC and Fox and does podcasts on investing. She is a speaker at conferences such as Venture Summit, the Women in Tech Summit, RoboUniverse and Women's Innovation conferences, and also mentors at XRC Labs, Grand Central Tech, The Vinetta Project and MenHERnyc. She is a regular judge for the Wharton Business Plan Competition and sits on the Board of the Penn Design School. She was a media executive at Time Warner and NBC Universal and a practicing corporate lawyer. She holds a BBA (business) degree from the University of Michigan and a law degree from the University of Pennsylvania.

Letter No. 6

Nadezhda Robinson, Founder of WEI-UK Consulting

Dear Female Founder,

I can't promise you that it's going to be fun, but it will be most certainly worth it.

I think this is a line from a film whose name I can't remember, but nothing is more fitting for the journey you are about to make!

I started my current business 6 years ago, but I have been an entrepreneur all my life. I remember distinctly that I already knew as an 8 year old that I wanted to be my own person, answer to myself and make my own money.

In my teenage years, I was pretty uninspired by the £5 per week pocket money my mum would give me. So I lied my way into an interview at McDonald's for a job that paid £3.20 an hour. I was underage, but ready to work. In fact, I was so determined to have my own money and to make my own choices that I somehow managed to secure myself a role serving burgers. That was 6 months before my 16th birthday.

Now trust me, starting off at McDonald's is no easy feat. People look down on you and respect is hard to come by. I did some dirty jobs, scrubbed toilets and cleaned up after others who barely looked at me or acknowledged my presence. Yet, to this day I will always say it was the best job I ever did and I highly recommend it.

I certainly learned who I could NOT be, but it also gave me respect and compassion for the people who do the jobs we look down on. This compassion has served me well in managing and maintaining a loyal team around me.

In the last 4 years, I have frequently considered self-diagnosis for schizophrenia, because the highs and lows come fast and furious. Stability of mind and feeling in control of situations became things of the past.

Decisions sometimes seem to mean life or death for your company, and the gravity of this will weigh heavily on you. There will be sleepless nights, when your mind seems to be a complete separate entity – engaged in a relentless conversation, which you cannot stop.

Once you employ staff, there is a constant worry, which you need to learn to live with: Can I pay them? Am I good enough as a leader?

You are not always sure if you are doing the right thing and sometimes – it turns out – you didn't. But in the grand scheme of things, all decisions are right.

You will also worry about the risk you take. You will worry about not being able to pay your bills, and being left behind as your friends progress in their careers, whilst you seemingly struggle to make it through the day. On some days, you might hate the business. On others, you might lack the strength to get out of bed. On many occasions, you might feel an urge to cry.

Now you're wondering why you should even be doing this, right?

Well, the answer – in my opinion – is simple: There is nothing else in the world I would rather do, nothing else I can do and nothing else I will do.

I'm driven to be an entrepreneur like some people are driven to write, run, or eat chocolate. It is what I was created to do. For all the hardships you must endure, there is nothing more rewarding than the process of bringing an idea to life, after you believed so much in it that you decided to take it from the world of the formless and bring it into the world of form.

There is nothing more life affirming and mind blowing than knowing that you are a creator. And that the world was a blank canvas until people like you had the courage to paint it with a kaleidoscope of colours, some more intense and long lasting than others, but no less meaningful and vibrant.

To be an entrepreneur is to be a creator of the highest order. It is belonging to the 1% of the population, that stands on the edge of the precipice, somewhat afraid to step out into the unknown, but much more afraid to stand still and be devoured by a life of regrets and maybes.

Being a female founder definitely comes with some additional challenges to our male counterparts. To name a few: a lack of role models, sexism, not being taken seriously, having to be 'nice', and difficulties in raising funding.

But every dark cloud comes with a silver lining. As female entrepreneurs, we add our own special blend to whatever we do, and it's that blend which can make us as successful as our male counterparts. So be secure in your role as a 'female' founder, it is part of the unique selling point of your success.

My experiences have been gritty, dirty and raw. They have tested me in unimaginable ways, constantly forcing me to dig deeper and fight a little harder, they have forced me to see myself for who I really am, a rather badass and resourceful kind of chick. I now own my title as *Managing Director*, rather than referring to myself as Marketing Director, like I used to do, because I was worried about whether people would take my business seriously, if they knew that I was the boss. Turns out that they do, and I am the boss, because I have earned the title. I will never underplay myself again.

The reality is that those who become successful only do so, because we are relentless in the face of constant challenge, change and adversity – all of which make the success even sweeter once we arrive. One word of advice here though: don't forget to celebrate all your successes along the way (there will be many) and don't focus too heavily on your perceived failures (there will be many).

So my dearest female founder, I have been thinking for weeks what to share with you in this last paragraph and I have decided to share one bit of wisdom inspired by Chimamanda Ngozi Adichie:

"The difference between those who dream about becoming a female entrepreneur and those who become one is simply that the latter tried."

In this life, I have learned that you should always *try* and then *do*. It is the common thread that has run through my life, even though I'm frequently just as afraid of failure as anyone else. I have always thought to myself: just *try* and see what happens.

So here is my parting advice to you: wake up tomorrow and *try!* Great things are waiting for you.

Love,
Nadezhda

About the author:

Nadezhda Robinson is a British entrepreneur based in London. She is the founder and Managing Director of WEI-UK Consulting, a company she started after being tasked to launch China UnionPay (China's National Bank Card System) in the UK in 2010, which facilitated the spending potential of Chinese consumers and added millions to the UK economy. Subsequently, she launched MINT, Europe's only accredited Chinese language lifestyle magazine, attracting China's A-list celebrities such as Li Bing Bing and Kris Wu to its front covers, whilst providing China marketing consultancy services to international brands like DeBeers, Vertu, and Coach. A serial entrepreneur with a proven track record, she is now looking to grow her entrepreneurial portfolio with the launch of www.mintstyled.com, a China-focused fashion and lifestyle eCommerce platform. Nadezhda is also working on her first not-for-profit education programme aimed at encouraging 16-18 year old girls to consider entrepreneurship as a viable career path.

Letter No. 7

Paulina Sygulska, Co-Founder of GrantTree

Dear Female Founder,

Nice to meet you! My name is Paulina, but most of my colleagues and friends refer to me as 'Pow' – a nickname that was officially invented by a random guy I met at a tech conference after-party, who ended up becoming my co-founder and later on my husband. KABOOM. Who would have thought!

I've always been led by an adventurous spirit, but if someone were to have told me years ago that I will have a substantial business with substantial earnings, a team of thirty people in a cool office building in Central London, as well as a non-negligible impact on the lives of people both within my team and outside of it... I would have seriously hesitated to believe.

But it would have been the voice in me that speaks from a place of fear. I would have felt that this kind of future isn't something I should have access to. Not given my irrelevant university degree, emotionally troubled youth and living a childhood focused on fulfilling everyone else's expectations, which made me realise that I had no idea what I wanted to do in life.

If you feel you can relate, then I would like you to start working on precisely this belief. You are worth all this and much more. How much more we will learn when one day you will feel ready to write a similar letter to your friend, daughter or another female founder.

For now, this is my first and most important request which stems from how much I care about you and all other women who choose to take their life in their own hands: during the days, months and years to come, I will need you to gradually change your self-perception. Nothing in the world will help you career, relationships with people, and life in general as much as doing that.

And in case this sounds cheap to you, we are not talking about the empty arrogance of Big Brother participants, who are looking to become the next Sophia Loren the moment they exit the show. This is something else entirely. I'm talking about the confidence that will push you through repeated failure, being skint when friends are building successful corporate careers, the confidence of feeling completely comfortable about being different in your lifestyle and in your beliefs about work, and the confidence of making your own choices, taking full responsibility for them, celebrating them, or forgiving yourself fully for having taken them.

You have all of it in you. To envision and create your own universe and to invite others into it, so that, one day, it feels like all the doors are open and the universe is shaping itself around you. This very belief – that you deserve the great things that will come to you – will become a foundation of your success.

Other foundations will be willpower and relentlessness, or what Y Combinator co-founder Paul Graham refers to as 'an animal' in a business founder. If you are prepared to do anything necessary, and more, to achieve your goals, you will find that this attitude alone will bring you more financial success than anything else.

Very importantly, you will need to learn not to burn out and pay with your mental health in the process. Many of my friends went that one step too far and blocked most of their potential and creativity as a result. Here comes the good news though, it will get easier as your self-awareness and self-love grows. One of your key learnings on this front will be to focus on looking after your mind and body and replenishing your energy first when the going gets tough. The sooner you embrace this, the happier and more balanced you will be.

Your success will also come from your trust in people and the ability to learn from those you aspire to. But beware that this trust can be put to the test. I've once had a close friend betray me for financial benefit and that was a pretty challenging situation to deal with. However, those difficult experiences will play a big part in your growth, as will big opportunities and little miracles placed on your way, if you choose to notice and accept them.

Similarly to me, you may be an individualist and naturally operate best as a lone ranger. Paradoxically though, what's likely to bring you the biggest joy is empowering others. These days, seeing my team grow and achieve higher levels of mastery and responsibility genuinely fills me with awe.

But enough preaching! Let's bring this all back to you and where you are today. If no one in your family has been a real entrepreneur and the notion of being in charge of a company seems scary and unattainable to you, stop worrying! Focus on things you have right now, and build on them. Your creativity, individualism and courage are more valuable for your career than anything you will ever learn at school or at university. Be proud of them. Be proud of the fact that you stand out, even though it tends to cause you pain or make you feel excluded from some social circles.

Don't forget it's your inner wealth that will form the foundation of your material wealth one day. That's why the best thing you can do now is to invest in your inner growth. This means becoming a fuller, more conscious person. It also means being grateful for your struggles and imperfections, as they will make you grow the most. Invest time and dedication to develop your spirituality, defining your beliefs and values. Learn from difficult relationships with other people, learn to forgive – particularly to forgive yourself – and learn to let go. Focus on what you can change and you will find how powerful you already are. As you grow older and become more experienced, your circle of influence will expand and you will have more and more impact on your community and the wider world. Get ready to handle this well.

More than anything, never lose your inner dreamer, wackiness and unconventional attitude.

I love you lots for embarking on this journey. We need more women like you. Think about this during those times you feel like you are alone. You are not alone. I'm standing right beside you.

Yours,
Pow

About the author:

Paulina Sygulska is an entrepreneur (also known as a 'saleswoman from hell') and a seed investor based in London. Originally from Poland, she moved to the UK to study at University College London (UCL). In 2010, she co-founded GrantTree, a niche fundraising consultancy, after spotting a gap in London's startup support ecosystem. In its first five years, GrantTree has helped over 500 tech companies in London and beyond raise over £30m worth of equity free funding from the UK government through R&D tax credits and grants. Paulina is also an innovator in the space of open company culture, which includes a transparent salary policy (also applicable to founders). When she is not growing her business ventures, she performs in various cabaret venues across London and organises the Unconventional Convention, a conference that combines quality inspirational content (think TED) with alternative entertainment (think Burning Man).

Letter No. 8

Rachel Lichte, Co-Founder of Clarity Project

Dear Female Founder,

When I first got to Sierra Leone, I learned a new term in Krio: 'smohl-smohl' ('small-small' in English).

'Smohl-smohl' seemed to be the unofficial motto of the country, applied to government and development in the same way as it was applied to dinner or transportation. I used to wonder if it was helpful in its practicality and honesty, or if its topical ubiquity dampened aspirations and held people back. But by the time I worked with a village to start a responsible diamond mine in Sierra Leone, the answer was obvious. There I learned that you have to start somewhere, and move forward little by little: 'smohl-smohl'.

Perhaps some relevant background would be helpful: it was 2001 and I was 18. I backpacked across the country of Costa Rica with an outdoor education program. We started out hiking through banana plantations, initially a wonder, given I'd never seen bananas growing before. Then I started meeting the workers who were working so hard, getting sick, and staying so poor. And after hiking a few days through these plantations, we came upon the distinct divide between the toxic banana plantation and the lush rainforest; only in the latter could we drink from streams.

In the rainforest, I met people, who found so much of what they needed from the natural land. There was a stark divide. It revealed that my choices

– as seemingly simple as a banana – affected the environment and people around the world. With a newly articulated belief that nobody should suffer for another person's lifestyle choices, I started on a path to connect responsible products with community and environmental benefit.

Fast forward a few years and I was working with non-profit organizations in international development and sustainability. I started working in marketing and brand strategy for mission-driven companies, causes and Corporate Social Responsibility programs, where I learned more about those companies that were in business for social and environmental benefit.

During this time, in 2009, my friends started getting engaged. And whoa, diamonds represented the most heinous gap between source and consumer, as countless people suffered over generations for this luxury. I felt vehemently against diamonds, and this drove me to learn more. I learned that despite the dark past and persistent problems in the diamond industry, most people in impoverished diamond mining regions rely heavily on the industry for work. Losing that financial foundation, without alternative job opportunities, would exacerbate their poverty and insecurity. This changed my mind about diamonds completely, and started me on what became a 6 year journey.

So in 2009, two friends and I co-founded Clarity Project, a jewelry company committed to using fair diamonds, gems and metals in order to support community development in diamond mining regions. We would prioritize small, African diamond sources in order to support and scale good practices. And we would use our brand and portions of our sales to support education and adult literacy in mining communities.

We started with very strict standards, too strict in fact. We had such limited inventory of diamonds that our strict standards would get in the

49

way of moving forward, which was necessary to achieve the progress we sought. We stuttered for a bit, but we decided that *we had to start somewhere.*

We would sell the best we could find and we would be fully transparent with our customers. In doing so, we could build a business through which we could improve our sourcing. Eventually, Clarity Project couldn't keep up with consumer demand, as materials for the products we wanted to create didn't yet exist at scale. This spurred me on to grad school and back to Sierra Leone to more readily understand the impacts and opportunities, the power dynamics, and the skills and resources needed to enable communities to benefit from their natural wealth.

Along the way, I learned that many miners held great pride in their knowledge of the land, mining, and their family legacy, but they experienced destruction, inequity, and a systemic inability to leverage work into wealth. I learned that 20% of the world's diamonds are mined by individuals or small groups in surface pits (called artisanal mines, similar to smallholder farms). I learned that miners felt stuck. And I learned that it was possible and desirable to make small changes in artisanal diamond mining operations that could positively impact communities and reduce environmental degradation.

In 2013, we worked with a village in Sierra Leone to start an artisanal diamond mine for community development. We mined in a way that exceeded a new third-party certification for social and environmental performance. We focused on health and safety, labor standards, environmental responsibility, community involvement, and accountability.

We started with land reclamation in mind, using a mining technique to ensure that precious topsoil wasn't lost to the river. We provided gloves and boots, first aid training and a nurse. This took time. We weren't perfect, but it was working. Soon, the number of bikes at the site started to multiply as our workers could afford bikes. They started their own small savings groups. We could not have done this on day one.

In the summer of 2014, after piloting these mining operations, we were planning to replicate our practices at other mine sites, but the Ebola outbreak made areas inaccessible and the work implausible. Over the next few months, the acceleration and repercussions of the outbreak shook the foundations of the communities, the country and the trade. And I made the hard decision to step away from Clarity Project.

What I initially saw as something that held people back – 'smohl-smohl' – proved to be the only way forward. We started somewhere, and had a goal in mind, but we listened in order to learn the best way forward.

As founders we can (we must!) envision the future of our company, but we must honor each step we take to get there. 'Smohl-smohl' is not the same as slow. Rather, 'smohl-smohl' means intentional progress, and in doing so it factors in the need to take in new information and adjust along the way.

While I don't work for the company that I co-founded anymore, I find that I still try to keep these lessons resonant in my mind. There is no 'perfect'. Start somewhere. Then move forward. Smohl-smohl.

Sincerely,
Rachel

About the author:

Rachel Lichte is an American creative strategist with global experience in sustainable value chains, design research, social enterprise strategy, and international development. She holds an MBA and a Master of Environmental Management degree from Duke University and has focused her career on integrating social impact with business value. In 2009, Rachel co-founded and led Clarity Project, a fine jewellery company with a bold mission: to leverage the power of the diamond industry to support development in impoverished diamond mining communities. She led a team of 39 people to develop an artisanal diamond mining operation in Sierra Leone, West Africa, with parts of the company's profits being used to funding education of 1,000 primary and 300 adult students in Sierra Leone. Despite their initial success, operations had to close down in end 2014 due to the Ebola outbreak.

Letter No. 9

Hephzi Pemberton, Co-Founder of Kea Consultants and Founder of The Missing Middle

Dear Female Founder,

Well done for stepping out and founding your own business. It is not easy; it takes guts. People will often think that you are a little crazy. That's a good thing. It's a sign that you are taking risk and you are innovating. If everyone agreed with you, then everyone would be a founder.

I started my first business, Kea Consultants, in the midst of the financial recession in 2009. It wasn't what anyone around me expected, particularly as I had previously worked at Lehman Brothers and narrowly avoided the fallout caused by their bankruptcy by a matter of weeks. It was a time when people were playing safe and cautious, not bold and courageous.

The question I asked myself was: how much have I got to lose? I'm 24, I have a good degree and some work experience. If me and my co-founder couldn't get something off the ground in a year, then we would go back into the job market at a tough time, but it was unlikely to be any worse than the present. I also had a deep gut feeling that this was a good time to start a business; even if it didn't work out, I would learn a lot.

The conditions were right on many other levels: I respected and got on with my co-founder, I had some savings from my banking bonus to use as

53

startup capital, I had a decent network and knowledge of the industry we were building the business in, and I had enormous amounts of energy.

Do not underestimate this last point. Starting a business takes energy. It is incredibly important to keep your energy levels as high as possible by looking after yourself in all the basic ways. Work out how much sleep you need and make sure you get it. Do whatever exercise you enjoy most – it needs to be energising, not draining. Spend time with positive people who motivate and encourage you, and nourish your body with good food. In the beginning, I lived off a fairly bootstrapped diet of homemade soups and salads, which served the dual purpose of saving the pennies and the (bodily) pounds.

Something I wish I had known earlier and have learnt the hard way – a highly effective teacher – is that your gut is your greatest guide. As someone who is predisposed to rationalising and analysing situations, this doesn't always come naturally. Although I have always believed in 'listening to your gut', I didn't practice as attentively and mindfully as I could have done in the early years of the business. There was a lot of steamrolling through situations, which did not lead to my best work or my most harmonious relationships.

I found that incorporating prayer and journaling into my daily routine were two of the best ways to tune in with what was going on inside me. This then allowed me to make the decisions of the day.

It was on one such morning in May 2015 that I had a very deep sense that my time at Kea was coming to an end, and that I needed to explore ways to exit. That was quite a scary realisation to have, as I was five months pregnant and intended to return to the business after nine months maternity leave, as my co-founder had done the year before. However, I couldn't ignore that little voice deep down inside of me and I'm very glad

I didn't, because exiting my first business has become the launchpad for my next business.

It is no shock to hear that your business will be like your baby. Especially at the beginning, before you are making money and can have some of your evenings and weekends back. Those first few months are as demanding and tiring as a newborn child. However, do not confuse the two. I had my first baby in 2015, after five years of running Kea full-time. I was fortunate enough to have an amazing co-founder who was at a similar life stage to me. We had shared openly our respective desire for families. In fact, we wrote 'babies' into the business plan from 2013 onwards. We decided that we would take turns to try and get pregnant and allocated ourselves a year each for that specific purpose.

Looking back, planning this seems bold and to some it might sound totally nuts – but it worked. We were both truly fortunate to become pregnant within our allotted year. We adjusted our shareholders agreement to include a maternity leave policy for us as founders and gave the whole thing the same level of thought and attention as we would with any other major strategic decision within the business.

On an emotional level, however, I was quite concerned about how having a real baby might take away from my business baby and I wrestled with this emotion for several months. In the end, I rationalised it in a very similar way to how I had done with starting the business. What was the worst that could happen? Yes, I might be out of the 'market' for a few months, but there are always ways of keeping in touch with people and remotely managing work. Yes, I might not be able to do all the things I used to do before having a baby, but I would also be able to do new things and discover a whole new side of myself that I never knew existed.

With hindsight, I'm glad I swallowed the fear and took the risk. It has led to the most enriching stage of my life so far and rather than limiting me, it has expanded me more than I could have imagined. I think that's what taking a (calculated and thoughtful) risk does – it gets you out of your comfort zone and helps you grow. My advice to my older self, from where I stand now, is to keep doing that my whole life long. I invite you to join me in that quest for development and growth, beyond the comfort zone.

Wishing all of you every success, enjoyment, and fulfillment in your new ventures.

Hephzi

About the author:

Hephzi Pemberton is a British entrepreneur and angel investor based in London. After completing her bachelor's degree at the University of Oxford, she entered her professional career working for Lehman Brothers and Glocap Search. In 2009, she co-founded Kea Consultants, a niche headhunting firm that specialises in placing candidates into investment and high-growth organisations, which she quickly grew into a sustainable business. At the end of 2015, Hephzi exited Kea Consultants to pursue her next ventures. She is currently a co-founder of The Inspire Movement and the founder of The Missing Middle. She is also a Board Trustee of Resurgo Trust, a charitable organisation with the mission to help communities overcome social challenges through outstanding church-based social ventures.

Letter No. 10

Lauren Klein, CEO of Girlmade

Dear Female Founder,

Trust your instinct. It doesn't matter if you don't have those 5, 10 or 20 years of experience like other founders do. What matters is that you have a gut and you know how to trust it.

How can you learn to trust your gut? You build alignment. You find like-minded people; your tribe or supportive mentors and advisors who can lift you up and help you reach your goals. How can you find those people? Well, look around you.

When we are very young, our parents can be our biggest supporters. This is a great start, but they may not have the experience to guide you properly on business questions. My parents, for instance, were educators who taught me to believe in constant learning and develop a growth mindset. This proved to be incredibly helpful for my career in general, but their advice fell short when it came to helping me bring products and services to market. They didn't pay attention to the commercial viability of my inventions or business ideas; they viewed the world through the lens of research and training – a very different lens to the lens of commerce. After all, they never had to register a patent or a trademark in their field of work!

If your parents are not business savvy, then ask them to find other adults who are. You always want to seek doorways that you can step through and give it 150% when a good learning opportunity arises. Demonstrate your passion – not only through your words, but also through your actions.

When I was a young woman, I worked with the mayor and leaders from private and public sectors to organize events that benefited my community. During that time, I navigated complex enterprise-wide programs and projects in communities, learnt how to be highly patient and resilient, and developed a very good set of communication skills.

However, later on in life, I learnt that not all political waters can be navigated with those skills. On some occasions, I could have really used the help of more seasoned business executives, especially in the convergence of 'women in business' and 'investment'. I could have made better decisions, had I understood how investors think and fund. Now I know that using data-driven and financial-led presentations could have increased my impact. I also learnt that it's important to practice your pitch and request timely feedback so that you can shape and contour your messaging to the audience.

There is interesting research happening at Oxford University right now that focuses on the investors who are investing in women and girls. The researcher's name is Kelly Northridge and her interest in the field stems from her own experience as the COO of a woman-led, high-growth venture, witnessing the discrepancies surrounding angel and venture investments in women-led companies. Get yourself educated in this area, because this is the arena you are playing in and the struggle is real.

Another word of caution: Technology fads are just that, short lived. It is the media's job to make those technologies look 'popular', so don't get too caught up in keeping up to date with the latest platforms and tools, if you observe bugs and poor service using them. Most likely, these new platforms will be overpriced (remember they are startup businesses too, who are looking to make profits); and even if they are free, don't feel pressured to be on every platform, just because everyone else is using it. Stay the course. If you know that there is a better product and/or option that works for you better, then pursue that avenue.

Also, stick with your values and ethics when choosing support services and products for your business. There are a bazillion apps and tools out there and many of them will have alternatives that do exactly the same job. If you find a company or its leaders behaving in a douchey way, consider voting with your dollars and *not* purchase or use their services. Small actions and ripples can drive long-term change.

Speaking of values and ethics, at Girlmade, we believe in living by these laws:

1. Give generously
2. Be honest with kindness
3. Ask for help

Make sure that you are always giving more of yourself than you receive. Give graciously and often. Additionally, always ask and seek out feedback. When you ask for it, give permission to others to be honest with you, but ask them to do it in a kind way. Through this process you can embody the approach to feedback that you want to receive in return.

Lastly, ask for help. This is maybe the most important law. Asking for help is often hard, but it is critical to know when you are outside of your competencies and it is time to delegate; and doing so can turn into jet fuel and propel you to possibilities you never imagined.

Living by these laws will help you create a culture of trust, inclusion and diversity – this trifecta is paramount to business success. As you build your company, it is really important to be mindful of building its culture for longevity. Culture eats strategy for dinner anytime. Your talent acquisition strategy and your exit strategy will be dependent on this very important, but often overlooked piece of work.

It is not an easy task, which is why I highly encourage you to find your tribe. Network, seek out mentors and ask for feedback. Be an eternal learner as you gain strength through this process – especially when you create a personal board of directors and/or an extended fan, community or supporter base who rally behind you. Seek out like-minded women and communities who themselves rise by lifting you up.

That is how you build alignment with yourself and your gut, knowing exactly what to do next. Give it a try. It's amazing!

Yours,
Lauren

About the author:

Lauren Klein is the CEO and owner of Girlmade, a company designed to empower young girls and young women to play big. Girlmade operates from Reno, Nevada, and hosts monthly inspiration morning sessions as well as the Girl Empire conference which aims to empower young girls on building confidence in communication, social netiquette and pitching skills. Lauren has a strong professional foundation rooted in over 20 years of business experience with Fortune 500 and international corporations. She is also a leadership coach specialising in social business, communities and change management with experience as a strategic member of corporate leadership teams. Lauren is constantly seeking ways to foster connectedness among individuals, groups and teams via their goals, vision and purpose.

Letter No. 11

Agnieszka Nazaruk, Founder of Calisthenics Academy

Dear Female Founder,

Slow down. Take a deep breath.

I am so proud of you for being here, for showing up, for searching for answers.

This feeling you have inside tells you that there is more to life, and that you have tremendous potential. It's real. Hold onto it. I promise you, you are here to create incredible things in your life. And even though sometimes you feel lost, beaten up, lonely and not enough, I want to tell you: everything will be just fine.

During our lifetime, we do a lot of silly things. We chase money for the wrong reasons, follow fame, go to places we hate and do things we have no passion for.

Like many of us, you may feel like you need to live up to other people's and society's expectations; doing things you *should be* doing, instead of doing what you *want to do.*

After a while, you might realise that all you want is to be yourself and to follow your inner desires.

But it's not easy. It requires you to be brave, to stand up for yourself and to work on your inner self. Friends might try to drag you back to safety and call you crazy. You might hit walls and run out of money. You might start questioning and doubting yourself.

Most of the people around you are tempted to give up in this situation, but not you. You will learn to become stronger and better.

Eventually, you will discover a few things you wish you would have understood sooner.

1. Fall in love with yourself and follow what feels good

You are an amazing and unique person. You have talents, stories, experiences and thoughts that no one else has. You are here to share your gifts with others, to create tremendous value, to serve people while creating abundance for yourself, your family and others.

I know that sometimes you feel that you are not enough. Not good enough, not pretty enough, not smart or outspoken enough.

If you follow that negative voice in your head, it will make you doubt your gut, your decisions and yourself. It will unconsciously sabotage you financially and make you feel like you don't deserve success, like you have nothing to offer. It will want you to give up on your dreams and follow others.

Don't let it do that.

Instead, fall in love with yourself. Your face, your body shape, and the way you walk and talk. It's you, and you are so beautiful when you are yourself. Self-compassion is a skill. You have to learn to be able to endure all the ups and downs that life has to offer. When you do that, you will be ready to make decisions. Not out of fear, and not because you wanted to prove something, but because you decided to do what's best for you.

This is where everything starts. No one should ever tell you how to live your life. You are the only one who truly knows what's best for you. Look inside and ask yourself: What do I love doing? What makes me feel good? When do I feel in the flow? Then do that.

It's not as easy as it sounds. It requires you to get in touch with your emotions. You can do that through practicing mindfulness and meditation (Headspace, the meditation app, is a good place to start). When you do it sufficiently, you will discover a space inside you that you can trust, which is solid, which is you. Do whatever it takes to connect with yourself. Once you know what you want, go after it with power and focus.

2. Success is not what you think it is.

It has taken me a few long years to understand that following my own path and my own happiness is what really makes life worthwhile.

Overnight success does not exist. It takes years of *consistent, committed effort* to build something of value, whether that is your business or your own personal development.

Examine your beliefs regularly and learn how to get rid of those that don't support you anymore. Ask yourself today: What does success really mean to you and where do you want to be in one year, three years and ten years from now?

Find a mentor or a development programme, and read as many books as you can. 'Awaken the Giant Within' by Anthony Robbins has helped me tremendously. Exhaust all resources that are available to you.

3. Shitty things happen. A lot. And that's ok.

You will need to face a lot of tough situations on your entrepreneurial journey. Things will not go according to plan, projects will fail and some of your supporters will leave you. Don't be harsh on yourself; know that this is normal. Think about what you can learn from each experience. Note it down, and then move on.

At the end, life won't be at all as you imagined it to be.

So stop guessing and go experience. Breathe life in with everything it has to offer.

This project you have been thinking about for a while? It's time to make it happen. You are unsure or not feeling quite ready yet? Let me tell you, no one ever is.

Close this book and ask yourself: "What is one thing I can do today to push my dreams forward?" Now, go and do it. Do you feel the fear creeping up right now? Kick it in the ass. You will rock it, I know. That is just part of your nature.

And one day, you will sit in your rocking chair, look back at your life and cry. They will be tears of joy, gratitude, and an immense love for life. And you will remember that day when you decided to absolutely own your life.

I am so proud of you.

Love,
Aga

About the author:

Agnieszka Nazaruk is a Polish entrepreneur, who has founded several ventures: an IoT green-tech company, a growth-focused marketing agency, a successful not-for-profit organization, and a digital business in the fitness industry called Calisthenics Academy. With an academic background in psychology and management, she is naturally fascinated by the intersection of business, technology, and psychology – relentlessly learning about life, success, failure and what makes us all tick. She loves the challenging and dynamic startup environment and is very passionate about entrepreneurship as a tool to make an impact, solve problems and create value.

Part 2
LEARN

"Never stop learning, because life
never stops teaching."

Letter No. 12

Danae Ringelmann, Co-Founder of Indiegogo

Dear Female Founder,

My name is Danae Ringelmann, and I'm one of the founders of Indiegogo. We are on a mission to empower people to unite around the ideas that matter to them and together make those ideas come to life. We launched in 2008, and after nearly 8 years, I have learned quite a bit about entrepreneurship, our world and certainly myself. I wish you all the success in the world, as long as the definition of success to which you aspire is your definition; no one else's.

Here are two learnings I would love to share – both as an entrepreneur and as someone helping entrepreneurs making their ideas happen.

1. Know 'Your Why'

Entrepreneurship is hard. It is messy, chaotic and full of uncertainty. The only thing that can be certain about entrepreneurship is why you're taking the journey to begin with. So make sure that's certain – know *Your Why*.

And then love it and embrace it. Wake up every morning repeating it. For when you meet what feels like an insurmountable challenge or you face a seemingly impossible decision (which there will be many), *Your Why* will guide you around and through them.

Your Why doesn't make entrepreneurship easy; it just makes it possible.

So how do you know *Your Why?*

Ask: why do you want to start a business, what problem are you trying to solve and why is this problem so important? After every answer ask why again (like an endlessly curious toddler exploring how the world works). Keep asking yourself why until you get to an answer that is a belief – something you can't rationally prove. Just something deep down you know is true for you. Then stop. You have found *Your Why.*

For me, I started Indiegogo because I wanted to democratize access to capital and entrepreneurship.

Why? Because I saw ideas going unborn every day not for lack of heart and hustle, but rather for lack of knowing 'the right' gatekeeper.

Why did this inequity matter? Because I thought every person deserved a right to bring his or her ideas to life.

Why did I believe entrepreneurship was a right and not a privilege? Because I thought life should be fair.

Why do I think life should be fair? Well I just do. It's my belief. It's my *Why*, and this *Why* has gotten my co-founders and I through the toughest periods with Indiegogo, and continues to guide our mission and strategy to this day.

What's also interesting is that the most successful entrepreneurs on Indiegogo are often the ones that know and share their *Why* relentlessly too. Campaigns with a video raise on average 4x more than campaigns without. In their videos, entrepreneurs don't just talk about what they are trying to achieve and how they are planning to achieve it, but also why they are trying to achieve it, and why their success matters to the world.

2. Expect Resistance

As illustrated above, entrepreneurship is not a linear path. It never goes according to plan; what you end up building often looks very little like the original vision in your mind. So while the problem you are solving remains the same, how you solve it will evolve – and that's OK. That is how it should be. The evolution – while challenging – is actually the fun part too.

So how do you ensure that your solution evolves? Expect resistance in all flavors (rejection, ridicule, and even self-doubt) and then turn that resistance into opportunity.

When an investor tells you "No" or a customer says "I wouldn't use your product", don't be discouraged. Instead, respond with gratitude. Thank them for the feedback, and then ask what would make them say "Yes" or "Okay, I'll use your product"? Same goes for when someone makes fun of your brilliant idea, calling it "crazy" or saying "It will never work". It even applies to you when you are questioning yourself, your intentions and your own assumptions.

When you are ready to hear "No", be laughed at and to second-guess yourself, then rejection, ridicule and self-doubt turns into learning. And that learning turns into progress, because it is the learning process through which you will acquire the information you need to iterate, improve and get closer to making it all work. When you are not ready, then resistance just turns into defeat. Plus you miss all the fun of evolution too.

Like Ghandi once said, "First they ignore you, then they laugh at you, then they fight you, then you win." So expect resistance! You need it to succeed.

And this is also why we have built Indiegogo to be a learning experience for you to test your assumptions about your ideas and to gather feedback. No one knows with certainty if there is a market out there for a product, service or creative expression that doesn't yet exist – not you, not any investor, nor any one customer or fan.

The only way to know if your idea has an audience is when you start putting one foot in front of the other, and iterating your way to a sustainable value proposition based on feedback all along the way. A campaign on Indiegogo just accelerates this journey and iteration process.

In sum, if you know *Your Why* and expect resistance, then the only thing between you and entrepreneurial success is yourself. So keep going and enjoy the ride!

The world needs change. The world needs you to succeed. And when you do, we will all thank you for enduring the journey and making it happen.

Good luck!
Danae

About the author:

Danae Ringelmann is an American entrepreneur based in Silicon Valley. She started her professional career working for JP Morgan and Cowen & Co, but left the finance industry to change the finance industry. After obtaining her MBA degree at University of California Berkeley, she co-founded Indiegogo in 2007 with a mission to democratise fundraising. Since then, she has helped to propel the company into the world's largest crowdfunding platform. Danae was listed as a Young Global Leader in 2016 by the World Economic Forum and one of Fortune Magazine's 40 under 40 in 2014. She has been a lifelong supporter of her parent's brick and mortar business in San Francisco.

Letter No. 13

Anna Alex, Co-Founder of OUTFITTERY

Dear Female Founder,

A couple years from now, you will be as experienced as I am today, running your company with a wonderful team and potentially a wonderful co-founder.

A couple years from now, you might sit back and think about how it all started. In our case, we were just two women who wanted to change the world of menswear. We both had just quit our jobs; and there we were, cheering on New Year's Eve 2011, promising ourselves that 2012 would be our year... and it was!

Also, a couple years from now, you will probably find yourself wondering how on earth you and your team did it all. For us, it still feels unreal. In four short years, we made OUTFITTERY the market leader for personal shopping in Europe, we dressed 300,000 men in 8 countries, we have 300 employees, and have raised over 30 million Euros.

I could tell you how we got there. But if I were to tell you everything about the last four years, all the ups and downs we had to face, you would probably back off and never start your own company.

Sometimes, it is good to be slightly naïve and optimistic about the exciting journey that is ahead of you, so I won't take this away from you. Instead, I'd like to give you some advice that will help you overcome any obstacles along your way, and hopefully take away some of the fears you might have when it comes to kicking off your own company.

Here it goes:

1. Find a partner you can trust

For Julia and I, it was essential to have someone who you can talk to about everything. The small, the big, the odd and the funny things. It always gave me strength and trust, and let me look at things with a certain distance. Remember: a sorrow shared is a sorrow halved, and a joy shared is a joy made double! This person doesn't have be a co-founder, it could also be a mentor. The important thing is that you have a really good emotional connection and deeply trust this person.

2. Focus on one rock at a time

Women in particular tend to worry a lot about things that *could* eventually happen. Being diligent is a great skill, but worrying about more than one thing at a time is not productive. Make a list of things to worry about and then decide which is the most important. Then fully focus on that, solve it and move on to the next. As an entrepreneur you sometimes feel you have a thousand problems to solve at a time, but this is not true. There is always a priority.

3. Build trust

Trust is the most important currency in business. It might be odd to believe that – in a world of numbers and KPIs – trust is the essential factor, but believe me it is so important!

If you don't trust your employees, they will not behave like trustworthy people and will never grow to realise their full potential. The good ones will leave you and move on to a place where they receive more trust.

If you don't trust your investors, you will have a problem anyway. Most deals are based on handshakes and trust. Don't forget that you are in the same boat with them and you must want to make your company successful together. By following the trust principle, you'll manage to build a fantastic team of employees as well as a fantastic board of investors.

A side note: if you feel that you don't trust someone, chances are very high that this person doesn't trust you either, and therefore your path together won't lead anywhere. Get out as soon as possible.

4. Listen to your gut

Very often, the heart is smarter than the head. But, in our modern business world, we tend to forget this. It doesn't mean that you should not check numbers and KPIs or take an informed decision on things. It just means that you should listen to your gut feeling and find out why some things feel good and others don't. Whenever you're in doubt, listen to your gut.

5. You can do anything

If there is something you think you cannot do, you are wrong. There is nothing you cannot do. It may require help from others, it may take some time, it may not be easy from day one, but it can be done. It is as simple as that: know what you want to do, and then go ahead and do it. That's all there is.

All the best of luck!

Anna

About the author:

Anna Alex is a German entrepreneur and the co-founder of OUTFITTERY, Europe's leading online Personal Shopping Service for men. With an academic background in economics, she launched her professional career at Rocket Internet Berlin where she mainly managed high-profile projects at Zalando, Groupon and Dealstreet, developing online marketing strategies and new features for these companies. In 2011, she moved to Zurich to lead the IT/Product team of the Swiss group-buying market leader DeinDeal. In winter 2012, she returned to Berlin to fulfill her dream of starting her own company together with Julia Bösch, a colleague and friend whom she met during her time at Rocket Internet. The duo wondered how they could make shopping a less painful experience for men, pioneered online personal styling, and turned their idea into big business.

Letter No. 14

Anne Ravanona, Founder and CEO of Global Invest Her

Dear Female Founder,

Here is the thing. A secret you know deep down inside of you: You already have everything you need inside you to succeed and be a fantastic entrepreneur! From one global woman entrepreneur to another, I have 5 key pieces of advice to help you on your unique journey.

1. Be Yourself

My mother would often write those wise words to me, when I was younger. As Oscar Wilde put it *"Be yourself – everyone else is already taken".* In entrepreneurship, you really have the opportunity to *be yourself.* In fact, you owe it to yourself. The more authentic you are, showing the real you (yes, 'warts and all'), the better you will resonate with customers, your team, your investors, other stakeholders and most of all, yourself.

Being an entrepreneur, a change maker, someone who sees a problem they passionately want to fix and does everything in their power to fix it, takes a huge amount of energy. You will have many decisions to make every day, so you can't waste energy trying to be someone else, or hide behind a mask.

When you are authentic, your team will follow you and go the extra mile for you. Your investors will invest in you because of what makes you unique – your special mix of character, values, personality, experience, talents and passion. Your family and friends will enjoy your quality time with them, because you are the real you, at home and at work.

I wanted to be an entrepreneur since I was 17. At 21, I opened up a sales office for an Irish company in France, straight out of college, in an industry I knew nothing about. I changed sectors, roles, and professions every 3-4 years, honed 5 languages as the voracious, curious learner that I am. Then I decided to be true to myself and my passion: help women leaders in business reach their full potential and create more gender equality – my deepest value.

I founded Global Invest Her to help women entrepreneurs get funded faster through demystifying funding. Every day we change hearts, minds, and systems. We will not wait 80 years for gender equality; we are doing our part now.

2. Be Brave

Starting and running your own company is hard, but so worth it! You have to be brave enough to say 'No' to a steady salary, a clear career path and a stable life, as your entrepreneurial journey will be a roller coaster ride.

You may create new markets, products, services or ways of thinking, so be brave and stand by the decisions you make. Expect and embrace all the 'No's' on the journey. Embrace your mistakes, be brave enough to own them, fix them and move on. Don't beat yourself or your team members up about them. You have chosen the path of the pioneer, steering an uncharted course. When doubt rears it's ugly head (it will) and that little voice makes you lose confidence (it may), then it's time to....

3. Believe In Yourself

I know that's easier said than done, but if you don't believe in yourself, your products, cause, team, or the company you are building, why should anyone else? Trust your intuition and your inner voice. It is a powerful guide; ignore it at your peril. Dramatic as it sounds, it's true that when I listen to my inner voice and fully believe in myself, magic happens and I increase my impact on the outside world. When I don't listen to my intuition, I always regret it later.

You have more power than you can even imagine, so it's time to unleash it – 'feel the fear and do it anyway'. Doing a TEDx talk, being a keynote speaker at conferences and contributing to the Huffington Post shining the light on other amazing trailblazing women are things I strived for and made happen.

"What the mind can conceive and believe, it can achieve", says Napoleon Hill, and my mind is burning with ideas to amplify women's voices and gender equality so that we have the same opportunities that our male counterparts already enjoy. Follow your passion, believe in yourself.

4. Think Big

If you are going to build a company, you may as well go big! Whatever you are thinking, think bigger, and you'll be amazed at what you will achieve!

If you were thinking of selling in one country, think several. One product line? Imagine another 2-3 in your pipeline. Dreaming of big partnerships, key corporates, many users – multiply that 10x. That's how guys think, and guess what, they do it!

We need more women-led businesses with $10-100 million revenues and we need more women-led unicorns. We (women) are the biggest market in the world (bigger than India and China together). We control more than 80% of purchase decisions and will control most wealth in the coming years. It's time to show our true worth to the world. Everyone will benefit, because we tend to build companies that impact our families, communities, and countries on a wider scale. Let's amplify that. Join the club!

5. Ask For More Money

Last but not least, ask for more money! Especially when you are looking for funding, be sure to ask for at least 40-50% more. Investors tell me they usually have to reduce male entrepreneurs projections' by half and multiply women entrepreneurs' projections by many multiples.

If you don't ask, you will not get. I watch women entrepreneurs pitch all over the world and they tend to gravitate to the magic number of 500K (regardless of currency) while the guys ask for over 1 million. And guess what? It's *just as hard* to raise 500K as 1 million so you may as well prepare your pitch deck for the bigger number, and not have to raise another round 12 months later.

If you are reading this, you have made the decision to change the world for the better. Now be yourself, be brave, believe in yourself, think big and ask for more money. I can't wait to see what you achieve!

Warmest wishes,
Anne

About the author:

Anne Ravanona is an Irish entrepreneur based in Paris. She is the founder and CEO of Global Invest Her, focused on getting early-stage women entrepreneurs investor-ready and funded faster. A passionate women's advocate with over 20 years experience in global business, she spoke at TEDx on 'Investing In Women Entrepreneurs' and is a regular speaker on the topic at conferences worldwide to raise awareness and help change unconscious bias to break the 'Funding Ceiling' for women entrepreneurs. Anne contributes regularly to the Huffington Post, showcasing great women leaders through her Trailblazing Women series and was recently named one of '26 Great People Spearheading Change In Tech Investment 2016' and '100 Women In Tech Whose Names You Need To Know 2016' by Silicon Republic. She has a diploma in Global Strategic Management from Harvard Business School, an honours BA in International Marketing & Languages from Dublin City University and speaks 5 languages. Anne is also the mother of 2 great bilingual children, a 14-year-old daughter and a 12-year-old son.

Letter No. 15

Shefaly Yogendra, Entrepreneur and Advisor to Founders

Dear Female Founder,

"Revolution only needs good dreamers who remember their dreams", wrote Tennessee Williams.

But remembering your dreams is not enough. There is a journey of sweat, tears and toil, between dreams and their realisation. There will be exhilaration, there will be joy, there will be pain, there will be doubt. But that is your journey now. And on this journey, it is crucial for your fellow traveller(s), your fellow builder(s), your co-founder(s) to be the right person(s).

To know if someone is suited to be your fellow traveller requires a fine balancing act of judgement and risk-taking, between similarities we seek and differences that enrich us. This sounds easier than it is. Here is a framework, which I hope will guide your search for that fellow builder!

Values make a person. Values of co-founders should ideally be the same or at least be in alignment.

Stanford researcher Noam Wasserman highlights the differences between people, who want control, and people, who understand that some control may need to be given up to build and grow value. People also bring varying risk propensities and interest in social signals. These values directly feed into many things such as their expectation of remuneration and titles. It is important to understand where you stand on these crucial matters and where your co-founder or co-founders might. Alignment, or lack of it, can make all the difference between a dream realised and a dream shattered.

Aligned values may lead to shared **beliefs** and shared beliefs shape a company's culture. A company's culture has a considerable impact on its success, or lack thereof. For instance, it is important to agree upon core activities such as how you want to treat your customers and your suppliers. These beliefs are hard to assess by spoken words alone. If you have the opportunity to watch your potential co-founder in action, such as with people over whom they have power, you will learn a great deal about about them.

Skills are best if they are different or complementary. The decision-making processes can be whatever co-founders agree on, but it helps if the co-founders bring different domain expertise and skills, which together are the building blocks of the startup. Don't hesitate to do your homework here. Ask around. Ask their former and current colleagues, ask customers, ask suppliers.

Which brings me to **work ethic**. It is ideal, if co-founders share a work ethic. Some people emphasise hard work, others outcomes. A startup needs both hard work and outcomes. But it needs outcomes and growth milestones more than anything else. If a founder thinks hard work is substitute for results, it ain't gonna work! So it is best if cofounders are on the same page as to their work ethic and its purposiveness.

Much as we all love the story of the lone ranger, some of the biggest startup successes around us are founded on partnerships and access to valuable networks. **Networks** are best if different or complementary to maximise the startup's reach and access to customers, champions and investors.

A word of caution here – there is no guarantee that the co-founder actually delivers on the advertised beliefs, skills, or networks. This means you also need to think ahead and think clearly about how to monitor the venture's progress as well as individual contributions, some of which may actively be costing the business crucial time or money.

Above all, trust your instinct and your gut feelings. Not because you are a female and stereotypes tell us that we have some kind of sixth sense! But because you have lived a life, you have worked and played with people, you have relationships and friendships. All these experiences have given you a compass, a heuristic you can access without conscious thought. This gut feel can be valuable when all data points in one direction but some discomfort lingers and we cannot put our finger on the exact reason 'why'. Let nobody tell you that your gut is any less right than the data you have collected!

Dear fellow founder, as you forge your path in the wilderness of entrepreneurship, I sign off by quoting T.E. Lawrence: "All men dream: but not equally. Those who dream by night in the dusty recesses of their minds wake up in the day to find it was vanity, but the dreamers of the day are dangerous men, for they may act their dreams with open eyes, to make it possible."

May you be the dreamer of the day, the dangerous woman, who acts her dreams with open eyes and makes it possible!

Yours in female founder sisterhood,
Shefaly

About the author:

Shefaly Yogendra is a British specialist in decision-making and risk, a Board Director and a charity Trustee based in London. As a former founder and COO of a fine jewellery venture, she has valuable insights across the full value chain of a luxury brand. She has over two decades of commercial experience in corporate venturing, risk assessment and advising investors and startups. She has been formally trained in engineering and business, and has a PhD in decision making from the University of Cambridge. Shefaly combines her education with her experience of having lived and worked in three continents, to bring a unique perspective to startups in luxury and technology sectors. She is one of the FTSE Female Board Report's 100 Women To Watch in 2016. She is also a keen culture vulture, a curious reader, and a devoted practitioner of Pilates and Vinyasa Yoga.

Letter No. 16

Alexandra Gamarra, Founder and CEO of Usetime

Dear Female Founder,

You are about to start a great journey full of personal satisfaction. However, I feel the need to warn you that the road ahead is not full of roses. I started my entrepreneurial journey 12 years ago and it has been a roller coaster ride. You will need to deal with a lot of challenging situations with customers, employees and investors. The business world is full of battles to fight, but when I look back now, I am very glad that I decided to become an entrepreneur.

First of all, being a company founder has given me the opportunity to do things that I could have never done as an employee. I had the freedom to take a gap year to travel around the world with my husband and my little daughter while still earning an income. That was an incredible experience and is something that only entrepreneurs can do.

However, I also have to say that I work a lot more now than I used to work as an employee. Being an entrepreneur is a 24/7 job. I think about my business day and night (but I like it that way).

Before you embark on your startup journey, please reflect upon your priorities and your goals. If you are used to a 9 to 5 job right now, then be aware that there is no such thing like a schedule or a routine once you start your own business. Possibly, there will be no weekends and no time for socialising either.

Therefore, it is important to think about what you really want. Why do you want to start a business and are you prepared to make sacrifices? Holding off your hobbies for a while might sound doable, but being a founder will also have a big impact on your family life.

I have met several female entrepreneurs who forgot about their families on their business journey and who found themselves completely lonely when they finally reached their professional goals. Don't let this happen to you, it's not worth it.

But generally, it is true that you will have less time for family and friends. On several occasions, I had to go on business trips, when I knew that my teen daughter wanted me to be home. I felt very guilty about it, but at the same time I wanted my daughter to see and understand that her mom is a businesswoman – and businesswomen need to go on business trips sometimes.

I know it can be difficult to handle, but don't think that you have to shoulder everything on your own. Have an open discussion with your partner or other family members on how to manage family life and your business. Ask other female founders how they do it.

Please also invest time in learning about leadership, and how to develop better networking and public speaking skills. Building confidence to practice these skills is a daily task, but the good news is: our confidence increases as we expand our comfort zone and lose our fear of failure.

My first public speech was embarrassing, because I am a very shy person. However, the desire to establish my business pushed me to improve and after several attempts (or practice opportunities), I started to feel comfortable about public speaking. The more I practiced, the more my confidence grew. But that is not the only thing I gained. Putting myself out there has also allowed me to promote my business and given me access to a new world of opportunities, which leads me to my next advice.

Focus on selling your product. Sales is the most important part of your business. Work hard on developing sales, persuasion and negotiation skills, and do not be afraid to get out of the office and tell the world about your product or service. Dan Kennedy's books and constant research have helped me to improve my sales skills. By doing that, I was able to find the customers I needed grow my business continuously.

Creating some sort of balance in your life is also very important. I know this is not an easy task as there are always too many things to do, especially in the early stages of your company. So work on becoming more productive during working hours. This should help reduce your workload at nights and on weekends, and you can fit in some quality family time and social life.

Whatever you do, do something you really love, so that your mind and heart are fully focused on it. You are the soul of the business and it will practically become an inseparable part of you – for many years to come.

Enjoy the ride!

Yours,
Alexandra

About the author:

Alexandra Gamarra is a Colombian business professional and serial entrepreneur, based in Bogota. She is the founder and CEO of Usetime, a cloud-based application that contributes to increased business productivity, allowing companies to better manage remote projects and facilitate the implementation of telework schemes. Alexandra created Usetime at a time, when she was running an eCommerce business with a yearly turnover of over $1 million in the UK, but struggled to manage her staff who was based in Colombia. She won the Seedstars startup competition in Bogota and was one of the finalists the Seedstars World 2015 final in Geneva.

Letter No. 17

Jude Ower, Founder and CEO of Playmob

Dear Female Founder,

I am Jude, Founder and CEO of Playmob.

I am a curious person with a penchant for solving problems, playing games and helping others. That's me in a nutshell. Now I want to share some advice and learnings from my years of being an entrepreneur.

Even though I have always had an entrepreneurial flair, it still doesn't make things easier. Whether you are a risk taker or risk averse, going out on your own will inevitably throw challenges at you. Learning how to deal with these and 'get out of your own way' will be your biggest feat. But this is a constant evolving process; I am always learning and always will.

I hope some of what I have learnt so far will help you:

1) **Believe in yourself.** You have to believe in yourself before others will. I was lucky in the beginning to meet some amazing people who saw the potential in me – potential that I didn't see myself. Once you start believing in yourself, your ideas, your ability, you can start to create the movement you dream of; but it has to start from within.

2) **Shit happens.** It always has and always will do, to us all! Worrying about what could happen or what is happening will only set you back in other ways. Deal with things as they come at you and be

aware of what could go wrong. Have contingencies in place, where possible. As an entrepreneur you will get out there, be hasty and make mistakes. You are moving fast and inevitably, things will go wrong. Being able to learn from this, admit mistakes and move on quickly, will be your biggest defence. Don't think that everyone knows what they are doing and have their shit together; they are going through hell and back too.

3) **Speak to your peers, a lot.** The BEST therapy you can get is confiding in entrepreneurs who have been through what you have been through, or sharing your story with them. When you open up, others open up too. It is amazing what you learn, and how it will make you feel about your own stuff. You are not alone. I was very aware that, at events, I would bump into people and ask how they were doing, and the typical response was "Fine, great, yeah really good". But if I quickly said "Ah great, good for you, I have had the worst week", then, it all comes out. If something is weighing you down, you will feel relief, a hundred times lighter; sharing the burden will help you see clearly. As Einstein said "No problem can be solved from the same level of consciousness that created it." If you are facing a problem, get out and speak to people, get different perspectives. I started curating a book called Startup Secrets (www. startupsecrets.club) to address this issue. I want to help startups share anonymous secrets for startups to feel not so alone. So working in two ways, a therapeutic tool to share problems in a safe place and a place to read other's secrets and think "Well, they got through that, things aren't so bad!"

4) **Take time out.** We want to get things done quickly, and are impatient. That's fine, and totally normal. However, if you stop to smell the roses, a new perspective can help you solve problems, leap forward and think more clearly. As founders, with hectic days and nights, we feel guilty for taking time out, constantly thinking about

the workload that's piling up. But sometimes just taking a step away, even just going for a walk or to the gym, will give yourself a chance to recoup and get the energy to take on the next challenge.

As you can see, my advice isn't on writing a business plan or the best way to run your cash flow. That is stuff that can all be learnt. The biggest challenges you will face will be in yourself and how you deal with things. This is why I focus inwards, rather than the stuff you can see or have to do. Being mentally prepared and having a strong will, will allow you to take on anything – to face your fears and deal with the unexpected.

Remember, don't beat yourself up, you are doing a great job. YOU are changing the world and YOU had the balls to step up and do that. YOU are amazing.

I wish you all the best on your journey – enjoy it, learn lots, and make your mark on the world.

Yours truly,
Jude

About the author:

Jude Ower is a British entrepreneur who uses game play to make the world a better place. She is the founder and CEO of PlayMob, creating the world's first platform profitably connecting game mechanics to social good. She has been voted One to Watch in 2015 at the Talent Unleashed Awards judged by Sir Richard Branson, Top 100 Women in Tech in Europe, Growing Business 'Young Gun' 2012, and Shortlisted on Red's Hot Women Awards 2012 and runner up Young Entrepreneur of the Year 2012. She is a BAFTA games judge, member of UKIE (UK

Interactive Entertainment), and an avid speaker at various events such as Institute of Directors, MADE Festival, SXSW and Women in Games. Jude has also been awarded an MBE for services to entrepreneurship by HRH Queen Elizabeth.

Letter No. 18

Leila Holballah, Co-Founder of MakeSense and CommonsSense

Dear Female Founder,

I am half Lebanese, half Colombian. I grew up in Yemen, Greece and France. Today I live in Hong Kong. When I was young, I never dreamt about being an entrepreneur. It just appeared to be a natural choice after my studies. Together with Christian Vanizette, I co-founded MakeSense in 2010 and CommonsSense in 2011. Since 2012, I am part of a collective of entrepreneurs building the MakeSense ecosystem.

MakeSense is a community-driven and owned social enterprise that empowers citizens to create and develop solutions to the social issues of our world. Since its birth 5 years ago, MakeSense got 25,000 people engaged to enhance concrete solutions built by social entrepreneurs. So far, MakeSense is spread in 100 cities in the world.

CommonsSense is a community design and consulting agency that helps organisations embrace and apply meaningful community dynamics within their business.

Here are some of the things I have learned as a woman entrepreneur, which I would have loved to have known beforehand.

#people

I am convinced that sustainable success of a company lies within its team. People are my number 1 priority. Are they happy? Are they learning? Do they have everything they need to build their path within the company? Are the roles and contributions clear enough? Are they incentivised to surpass themselves? I have been told one day: "You are giving us clothes that are too big for us, we want to surpass ourselves to fill them".

Your co-founder is like a boyfriend/girlfriend:

- You need to share the same set of values in life.

- You should admire him or her.

- A look should be enough to pass on a message.

- You should be able to have tough conversations and be confident that you will find a solution together.

I have learned to be as clear and explicit as possible when I communicate. I do this to avoid any misinterpretation or misalignment of expectations, but be careful with the words you use. Using harsh and alarming words will only nourish stress and mistrust.

On the other hand, always celebrate good news and successes, even the small ones!

#business

Once you are clear about your value proposition and the concrete solution to the problem you have identified, just focus on that. Focus on delivering the best quality of your solution, focus on your beneficiaries and your partners, and only that. Don't spend too much energy looking around you. The more you show consistency and tenacity in the long run, the more people will follow you, even your competitors!

I have been asked so many times "What is your vision of the company in 5 years?" and I can only tell them where I *do not* want to go.

Sure, it is important to have a direction, but it is equally important to leave space for your project and your community to surprise you, and to take you to unexpected places, faster than you ever thought! For this to happen, you need to have the right attitude. Observe, listen and make space to support new ideas and opportunities. Watch the waves and ride them! Your role is to be the protector of the vision and mission.

#organisation

When you start your venture, you will take care of everything. This is the best school ever! However, soon enough your team will grow and you will need to ask yourself what the role is that you want to play in the project. You won't be able to keep on doing everything. Make it clear for you and your teammates, as it evolves with time. Co-design an organisation that would enable everyone to bring the best of him or her into the adventure.

When you start your venture, fast and furious, decisions will probably be taken quite rapidly. As more people join, decisions will have a larger impact. It is key to have a clear and explicit decision-making process. This does not mean the process has to be long and complicated. Just state precisely who takes the decision, why, how and make that transparent to everyone.

#you

Stay true to yourself! I am a workaholic and I like working on Sunday evenings. I admit it. It is a challenge for me to balance my private and professional life. But I am getting better at it, I think. I have learned to accept my way of life and stopped blaming myself. People around you might judge you, tell you that you work too much and that it is a bad thing. I thought about it and realised that no one was forcing me to work that many hours. It was my own happy choice to live this way, as long as this is not a problem for my team or my boyfriend!

One day, a friend has told me those wise words: a company has the qualities and vices of its founders. If you are aware of your vices, check if those vices have a bad impact on the company and get rid of them!

Ask yourself what recognition you are looking for. From who? How? In organisations where a financial exit is unlikely, this is a tricky, but key question to address – for those who started the company, but also for those who will join you and who be fully committed to the company. I feel very lucky to work with such genuinely committed people with whom we can discuss this topic with trust and no taboo.

Most likely, you have been told to look for mentors. My three mentors are friends of my age. Two are entrepreneurs and one is working in Corporate M&A. For me, a mentor does not need to be older and knowledgeable. He or she just needs to be a very good listener and someone who asks the right questions.

I will end with a feminist note. If you are a young woman entrepreneur, some male clients and partners might not take you seriously. Lean in! Recall your role in the organisation – especially if your co-founder is a man, but you are the boss.

Enjoy the ride and make the most of it!

Yours,
Leila

About the author:

Leila Hoballah is a Lebanese-Colombian-French entrepreneur based in Hong Kong. She is the co-founder of MakeSense, a worldwide community of volunteers, that helps social entrepreneurs solve their challenges, and CommonsSense, a consulting and design agency, based in Paris. CommonsSense helps organisations create and animate challenge-solving communities inside and/or outside the company to make them more innovative and more dynamic. Leila holds a masters degree in Entrepreneurship from ESCP Europe business school in Paris, where she co-founded the student association NOISE and co-launched the movement Disco Soupe. She was also part of the Expert Group on Social Entrepreneurship of the European Commission.

Letter No. 19

Bryony Cooper, CEO of IXDS Labs

Dear Female Founder,

When I became CEO of my first startup at the age of 26, I had absolutely no clue how much my life would change. My new colleague and co-founder had a vision, and I truly believed in it. Although I had never heard of a VC or an Angel (aside from celestial beings), the idea of being my own boss was quite appealing; not to mention the awesomeness of having 'Chief Executive Officer' printed on my business cards! Never mind my complete lack of experience and formal business education.

From the day we made the decision to pursue our startup idea, a Software as a Service proposition for private transport companies, you could say that things snowballed. I still don't know if it was luck, timing or just a great pitch, but we managed to raise money on our very first attempt. I contacted Seedcamp on the last day of applications and we were invited to the finals in Berlin days later – pitching to 100 business mentors and investors (i.e. men in suits). Only mildly intimidating!

I was one of about five women in the entire room. We didn't actually win Seedcamp, but to our surprise, an investor offered us €75,000 a week later on one condition: that my two co-founders and myself relocate from London to Berlin and join his co-working space. And so came the first major life change; I decided to not be scared of the great unknown and gave it a shot.

Running a startup is an exciting and challenging experience, and a constant roller coaster. The ups and downs *will* leave you exhausted, but I can guarantee, you will never be bored.

You have to really want it though. Being a founder requires you to be *all in,* because it's not going to be easy.

On some days, you feel like you can take on the world. When things are looking great for your company and an investor has just agreed to help you make your dream a reality, it's all too easy to overcommit yourself to results that, realistically speaking, aren't achievable without working 25 hours a day.

Beware, young Padawan... It is the investor's job to squeeze the best results possible out of you (some of them would employ whatever means necessary), but it is your job to keep your team and company flourishing, which you cannot do if you are overworked and buckling under the pressure.

Here are some things I learned along the way:

Don't bite off more than you can chew. It's hard to say no when you're offered the opportunity of a lifetime. Everyone is depending on you: your co-founders, your employees, your investors, and your clients. Your friends and family see you as the next Marissa Mayer and you are profoundly aware of that. Of course, you don't want to let them down. But remember...

Asking for help is not a weakness. Trying to carry the burden alone will only drive your stress levels through the roof and leave you closer to a burnout, and then you'll be of no use to anyone. If you really want to lead and support your team, know your own limits and listen to your body when it tells you that it's had enough.

Learn to delegate. You cannot do everything by yourself. As your company and responsibilities grow bigger each day, it just isn't sustainable to increase your capacity to that of 10 people. Surround yourself with a team who you trust to get shit done. Otherwise you will end up feeling more like you're carrying extra weight, when they should be making your life easier.

The world will not end if you take a sick day. Seriously, it might feel like everything will fall apart without you, but you'll find that your team can actually hold the fort while you recover from the flu. Have a little faith in them.

Over 4 years running my first startup, I experienced a lot of very difficult challenges. Going months without pay, working 16 hour days, giving up my idyllic London life for a strange new world, falling out with a co-founder, difficult investors, subtle sexism and making very hard decisions like having to fire people you've come to think of as friends. And man, was it hard! But without stepping up to those challenges, I wouldn't be where I am today.

At the time, I often felt like I was failing. Our numbers were never good enough, the bar was always set slightly too high. But looking back, I see a great success: we raised €2 million, won clients worldwide on 6 continents, built a team of 20 people and the company is still going today. With the lessons I've learnt, I've gone on to mentor various early stage startups, hopefully helping them to avoid some of the pitfalls.

Another revelation is that I am more resilient than I ever thought possible. I bet you are, too. Believing in something gives you great strength to keep getting up in the morning, even when it seems like the world is trying to keep you down. Do you remember that retro toy jingle, "Weebles wobble but they don't fall down"? Well, that's become my catchphrase. No matter how many knocks you get, keep on going.

You are already more impressive than you realise.

Yours,
Bryony

About the author:

Bryony Cooper is a British entrepreneur. She is the CEO of IXDS labs, a Berlin-based design and innovation platform for building connected hardware startups. Previously, Bryony was CEO of a B2B startup providing SaaS tools to transport companies; her first venture was a London web development agency specialising in SEO. In addition to coaching early stage startups, Bryony is an energetic public speaker, with a creative background in copywriting and online marketing.

Letter No. 20

Katariina Rantanen, Founder of CosmEthics

Dear Female Founder,

No matter how old you are when you start your first business, here are some thoughts from decade to decade, a word of encouragement and a friendly note on the path that lies ahead of you.

Teens: Hang out with your friends and build bonds that last a lifetime. Be silly. Don't worry about what other people think. Absorb the things from education with curiosity, and let that guide your thinking and learning. Don't stare at the grades and metrics. Aim at insight and understanding something new. See if there is an area that interests you in particular (maths, sports, science, nature, languages etc.) and be happy if you have an area of strength.

Twenties: Try different things, without aiming for a strict career after your studies or do something just to please someone else (your parents, for example, or because "this looks good on my CV"). Pursue fascinating things with curiosity. I was an investment manager, did PhD research and taught Entrepreneurship. I started my first company in jewellery design, expanded to perfume design and then went on to consulting. I learned a lot from diverse industries. Don't get stuck. Now is a great time to travel and live abroad. Explore and learn what drives you and what makes you tick.

Thirties: Immerse yourself into something that you are passionate about. What do you want to change? If you hate your job, leave. If you wished something was different, see if you can change it. Build something. Most importantly, don't do it alone. Gather the right mix of people around you to take the leap with you, if you can. If you can't find them (like me at first), give it time. Don't be fearful of making mistakes. Don't give up on your dreams. Fight for them, and pick a goal worth fighting for.

Problems will arise at each stage of your life, and the most important thing I have learned is to *not* keep them to yourself.

Lastly, I wanted to share some tips to help you sort these problems out:

Ask for help. The other day, I sought out a fellow CEO and had a heart-to-heart discussion on pressures of the job. Find people that are less emotionally engaged in your problem, and hear their proposed solutions. Sometimes just talking helps, and realising that you are not alone with similar thoughts gives a sense of relief. He gave me resources, practical advice and a sympathetic ear, which made a huge impact. Being vulnerable is human. Showing compassion is heartwarming. Remember to be there for someone who reaches out to you in return.

It's OK to make mistakes. If you never make any, you have just been playing it too safe. If you do blunder, give an honest apology, and do the right thing. If you fail at meeting your goals (in business or in life), see if you can push harder – or maybe you have been using a wrong approach? Try a new strategy. Hopefully, you can go through this with a mentor who can challenge you and guide you.

Be merciful towards yourself. A mentor and investor of mine, whom I admire strongly, told me once: "Forgive yourself each evening before going to bed. Challenge yourself in the mornings."

I hope this advice helps you on your startup journey.

Don't hesitate to reach out to me too!

Katariina

About the author:

Katariina Rantanen is an entrepreneur who believes in purpose-driven businesses that put mission and social purpose first. She is the founder of CosmEthics, a company that helps consumers make healthier cosmetic choices through a free application that reads product barcodes. A native Finn, she was brought up in the UK, and spent much of her youth in the US. She launched CosmEthics in 2013, after living in France for two years, where she did Ph.D research and perfumery work in Grasse. Katariina holds a masters degree in Entrepreneurship, and has worked in education (Assistant Professor), venture capital and business advisory roles. Her passion is promoting open data and helping people choose healthier cosmetics. She also promotes strict adherence to legal compliance in the EU regarding ingredients used in cosmetics. CosmEthics was chosen as the 'Hottest Lifestyle Startup Trend of 2015' by Forbes and has also received the IBM Cloud 'Entrepreneur Of The Year Award' in 2015.

Letter No. 21

Judy Liu, Co-Founder of Curiosity China

Dear Female Founder,

It is very important to have a coach, someone who can lead you to think in the right direction. However, not everyone is so fortunate to find someone who will listen and give advice, especially at a young age.

Building a project from scratch and growing your own company is the most rewarding professional experience you will have in your life, but it is also very challenging. I would like to share some important lessons that I have learnt in the course of my life. Hopefully they can help guide you on your journey.

1. Be confident

First thing: be confident!

If you work hard and have the right attitude, you will *always* achieve something. The magnitude of your achievements will depend on various factors, but everything will come when you are willing to work hard for it. Start somewhere and build things step by step. Try to be as efficient as you can. The more you do, the more your confidence will grow.

2. Speak up

My French husband used to say to me: "I think it's very hard to be a Chinese girl. You need to look pretty, have a good career, be financially independent, take care of your big family and, in addition, deal with male chauvinism in society."

It is true that the Eastern culture requires considerable effort from women to raise our standing in society. However, things are changing in the right direction. Ignore all outside influences. Always speak out and let others hear your voice and your opinion. That will truly help you get the respect you deserve.

3. Learn how to learn

Knowing how to constantly learn new things will pay off big time on your entrepreneurial journey. One of the main reasons why a lot of people choose to start their professional career at a large corporation is because of the training they would receive. However, gaining the capability to learn on your own is much more valuable and important than waiting for someone else to teach you.

When I started my own company, I was able to leverage my professional experience initially. But the scope of work was much larger than what I had to deal with in my corporate career. Handling marketing, sales, human resources, design a product from scratch, and understanding the mindset of engineers were only a few challenges I had to face. It was really continuous learning and practising new skills that allowed me to achieve things I would never have thought I was capable of achieving.

Now I know that we can only actualise our own potential, when we are able to direct our own learning. When I finally understood this, I also realised I don't have copious amounts of free time anymore to complete a proper study course on a new subject. I have to fit it into whatever else I was doing.

Therefore, treasure the time you may have now for learning and make good use of it. It will become the biggest luxury you can have.

4. Be brave like a child

Remember how we used to be when we were kids; not afraid of speed while skiing and not afraid of heights, when we wanted to climb a tree. Even at school or at the beginning of our careers, we did things without much concern. However, the more experience and responsibilities we get, the more we get bogged down with worry.

As adults, we *think* more than we *do*, which can hold us back tremendously. Don't get stuck in analysis paralysis. As women, we possess a great deal of emotional intelligence, so trust your gut feeling, be brave and make a decision!

5. Care about your team

The easiest way to build your dreams is to work with people you like and get them behind your vision. Women have a natural ability to gain trust from others. That is a big advantage! Use this natural gift to build a good team and take care of them.

Don't lose sight of yourself when the pressure is on. It is easy to become less patient or even a bit arrogant, but you can't lead your company, if people don't like to follow you. The biggest achievement for a startup team is to grow together and work coherently together to make things happen.

6. Don't wait for perfection

Almost all of my investor friends tell me: "As a female leader, the most common mistake is to make everything perfect rather than making progress."

Please don't make that mistake. Know what is 'good enough' for what you currently want to do and go execute it. Progress is only achieved by taking action; so don't wait for conditions to be 'perfect' to go after your goals.

If you really want to achieve something, you will always find a way. If you don't, you will find an excuse. Also, force yourself to think bigger and further. In the long term, there is hardly anything you cannot achieve. You don't need to be 100% ready, all you need to do is to make the first step today. The rest you will figure out.

It took me quite some time to fully understand the lessons above, but I am truly thankful for everyone who has influenced me along the way. I would be very happy, if my thoughts can help you a little bit on your own journey too.

Yours truly,
Judy

About the author:

Judy Liu is a Chinese entrepreneur based in Beijing. She has over 10 years experience in operations, business development and product management. In 2013, she co-founded Curiosity China, a digital and technology company for brands and agencies looking to leverage social CRM and digital marketing for Chinese consumers. Curiosity has created "CURIO", an exclusive bilingual social media CRM management tool to perform social monitoring, digital marketing activities and members management. After two short years, Curiosity China has grown to 35 employees who are working across four offices in Beijing, Shanghai, Hong Kong and Paris.

Letter No. 22

Kinga Jentetics, CEO and Co-Founder of PublishDrive

Dear Female Founder,

I am Kinga, CEO and co-founder of PublishDrive.

"I was born to make a difference with my work" – that is my life motto, which drove me to a life of being an entrepreneur. I always had a passion towards creative industries such as publishing and music, so there was no question for me where to focus my work. One day, I decided to take a first step and became a founder.

When I first created the company, I had no idea what I was signing up for. I was still a student, naive but excited about challenges. Starting your own company is like having a child. You can never be wise enough or prepared for everything that might happen.

With PublishDrive, I learnt how to pivot and move quickly. We developed software to help digital transition in a traditional industry by automating all parts of the ebook management process and helping content reach its global audience instantly.

I have learned lots of lessons in the past few years – many of which I wish I had known before starting on my journey. I hope they bring you the courage and motivation to continue:

1. Think big and be persistent

You probably have heard the sentence "You cannot do it, it is too big " or even worse "You are too small for that".

Trust yourself that your product can make a difference on a global level. Do not let anyone make you feel smaller than that. Even people you would consider potential customers may be hesitant to use your product – and you may never know why. However, if you are persistent and you have a product that creates value in someone's life or work, they will find you anyway.

This attitude helped me get in touch with the management teams of Apple, Google, and Amazon, and resulted for PublishDrive being one of the only 10 companies globally trusted by Apple. It wasn't luck. I simply 'stalked' the right people and my co-founders, Robert and Adam, and I worked extremely hard to build an awesome product, show traction and document processes on over hundreds of pages.

So I would rather change the sentence of non-believers to "You won't do it, if it is not too big".

2. Sharpen your people skills and know when to say 'No'

Trust is the foundation of teamwork; you cannot change the world alone. You have to trust your team and your partners unconditionally, and do not be afraid of change. Change is good. It brings you new vibes and ideas, even if it feels unknown and risky in the beginning.

With PublishDrive, we learnt to say 'No' to partners or team members who could not bring value to the company. This, of course, challenges your emotional strength. How could you identify that someone does not contribute enough value? Trust your feelings and sharpen your people skills – it is the most important skill that you will need as a founder.

3. Go to market as early as possible and start lean

Do not wait too long to show off your product to early customers. Find someone who is willing to pay for your product and find out why. Is it your personal charm or do you offer value to them? Identify those values and develop scalable solutions around them. Even though you started a company to make a difference, you have to be profitable to do that on the long term.

We started PublishDrive in a very lean way. We acquired our first paying customers without any software and did the hard work manually. This way, we talked to our customers a lot and enjoyed every conversation with them, which gave us great insight into our customers' needs. Our product was therefore developed in conversation with our customers and led to a real solution to their problem.

4. Build relationships and nurture them

If you find your first customers, you can validate your idea. But this is just the beginning. You have to keep them in the long term – that is where the hard work starts.

With PublishDrive, we found that the customer lifetime cycle is more than two years. This means that customers stay with us for quite a while, once we have gained their trust. Even better, by building meaningful relationships with them, we were able to turn them to evangelists for our company.

When we launched our affiliate program a few weeks ago, we started to send out customised offers to our appreciated partners, which resulted in new customers without any time-consuming campaign or costly marketing effort. Relationship building is not something you can scale easily, but it also cannot be copied easily. If you do it right, it becomes your secret weapon.

5. Hire people, but know how to hire right

As a founder, you will have to do many things you never done before. Get acquainted with accounting, operative sales or even basic development.

Sharpening your skills in many areas will give you an overview of how the business is working, but you will reach a point when you need to hire people for specific tasks. Build your skills in recruiting the right people and assessing your team. It will grow you into a better C-level executive and you will learn how to delegate tasks more effectively.

When you hire, do not fall into the trap of hiring fast. Focus on quality people who can bring a difference to your organisation and shape your culture with you. You do not just need employees in the beginning; you need partners and people who are freaking good at things where you are lacking skills.

I am sure that you can also tell me a few enlightening experiences and useful tips, so I encourage all of you to start a conversation about what worked for you. As a result, us female founders can make a difference together.

Best,
Kinga

About the author:

Kinga Jentetics is a Hungarian entrepreneur based between Budapest, London, and New York. She is the CEO and co-founder of PublishDrive, a software company that helps digital publishers increase their ebook sales globally by distributing their ebooks to more than 400 stores in 72 countries, including Amazon, iTunes, Google Play, Barnes & Noble and Kobo. PublishDrive is also an Apple Approved Aggregator company for iBooks. Kinga won first prize at the pitch competition at Northside Festival, New York, in 2015 and was a finalist at the first Central Eastern Europe Startup Women Competition in 2014. She holds a PhD degree in marketing management from Corvinus University of Budapest and is an active ambassador of women entrepreneurship.

Letter No. 23

Roberta Lucca, Co-Founder of Bossa Studios and WonderLuk, Founder of BOLDR

Dear Female Founder,

When I was younger, I had no idea how much I could change my life's course with certain decisions that 'the wise' would find reckless or way too risky. Ten years ago, I crossed the Atlantic Ocean from Brazil to continue my life in the UK. I founded and built two successful tech companies, and still managed to keep up with my loved ones somehow.

Normally, I'm quite critical with myself, but today I wanted to take a moment to be grateful, and share some thoughts with you.

Having the guts to change, when you are not doing what you love, is a rare gift.

It demands deep self-awareness, everyday practice. It requires you to *zig* when everyone else is *zagging*. It can be isolating, because you are not fitting in most of the time. You are not being part of the rat race, like most people.

But change is what keeps us young at heart. It keeps us being marvelled by the world around us. Changing is learning. Learning a new way to do things you already know, learning brand new things, being stupid again. Willingness to change, and let go of what's not needed, is what truly keeps moving us forward.

In fact, these are the fundamentals of entrepreneurship. And something that may well help you have higher chances to impact the world with your vision and determined execution.

It is not as easy as it sounds. Tough moments will happen on this rollercoaster ride that is your life as an entrepreneur. These moments transform into lessons you must never forget. Here are mine:

1. Be careful of the 'experts' you encounter along the way. In the startup world, everyone has an opinion and a piece of advice to give you. Ultimately, you will discover that only a few of them really matter to you. You discover your own truth.

2. Build your network. Not only build it, nurture it. Engaging with other founders who are on a similar journey will make you feel at home. Find a trusted environment where you can exchange contacts, learnings and even do business with them in the future.

3. Stay focused and positive. Whatever happens while you are building your startup, product and team, you need to keep two thoughts in your mind: "I believe I can change the world for the better" and "I will make it happen".

4. Surround yourself with people who love what they do. Self-awareness is underrated. Stay away from people who can't take initiative, talk too much and do too little, or over-analyse everything.

5. Timing is key. Being a perfectionist will only make you a worse leader and a massive procrastinator. You will have to make decisions when you don't have all information you need. Decisions like replacing people in the team, pivoting your strategy or even pressing the reset button.

6. Get an executive coach or use an app for that. Like great dentists, they are difficult to be found and if you do find one, you will probably not be able to afford him/her. That is why I started my third venture. BOLDR is a tech startup with a vision to democratise coaching, making it affordable and convenient to everyone. Why do you think the best elite athletes have coaches? Because coaches can really help you move forward in all your stuck moments and allow you to make a leap in your performance as a founder, leader and human being.

7. Exercise and eat well at least five days a week. I really mean it. Do it. Just do it. You can't imagine how your energy improves when you create the habit of exercising. Too difficult? Not enough time? Start simple: download a fitness app like 8fit or Runtastic Results and get a virtual personal trainer who helps you with a 10 minutes gym session that you can do in your living room.

8. And never forget: be grateful, every day. No matter how you feel at the present moment, always remember to look at what you have achieved, the courage you had to do things others did not. Remember all the individuals who helped you along the way. Say "Thank You" to them, from the heart.

Your perseverance, your resilience, openness to change and zest for life are powerful and contagious. Those qualities will take you much further than you can possibly imagine right now, and may even inspire many people along the way.

Yours truly,
Roberta

About the author:

Roberta Lucca is a British-Brazilian serial entrepreneur based in London, with a passion to drive change through Blue Ocean type of tech businesses and products. She co-founded the BAFTA-winning scale-up Bossa Studios, growing the company from zero to millions in revenue and wowing influential YouTubers with hits like Surgeon Simulator. She also co-founded WonderLuk, a '3D printing platform for design lovers', now with a community of 40+ designers and clients such as the Science Museum London and the V&A. Roberta has been voted 'Top 35 Women Under 35' by Management Today, Top 30 Women in Games, Influential Tech Leader, and was everywoman's Entrepreneur of the Year finalist. Prior to entering the entrepreneurial world, she spent 12 years creating disruptive products at corporates such as Nokia/Vertu, and the world's second largest commercial TV broadcaster, Globo TV.

Letter No. 24

Servane Mouazan, Founder of Ogunte

Dear Female Founder,

You are on your way to make big changes in the world, because you know it shouldn't stay this way. But if you think you can save the world through social entrepreneurship, then I'm bound to tell you: you probably won't.

Don't be discouraged just yet, because I think you shouldn't worry about changing the world in the first place; and I am going to tell you why.

Do you sometimes feel a huge disconnect in the world, in your community, and even within yourself?

This is because you live in a world that is driven by the economy of loneliness – an economy where your own body and soul, communities, and the future of our world are misaligned and disconnected. And this economy of loneliness is what makes a lot of social entrepreneurs fail. If you keep contributing to this economy of loneliness, you will not maximize your impact, let alone make an impact. But you can act now to avoid the worst.

As a young adult, I had a strong desire to support community activism, and to help people to have a local impact. My company Ogunte was established in 2001. It came out of my interest in creating social change through activism and my will to initiate meaningful dialogues among community leaders.

Little by little, I started to engage in conversations with these leaders from all around the world. They were teachers, musicians, developers, entrepreneurs, campaigners, and funders. We were united by the knowledge that – to create change – you need to put your head above the parapet, break silos, and act with the future in mind.

Back then, I didn't know how I could implement all these ideas, but I knew for sure that I had to create a space in which I could experiment and grow a network of like-minded people. Then one day, I realised that the people attending most of our workshops and public events were mainly women. They were at the nexus of many worlds, no longer NGO's, but not yet businesswomen. These women were social entrepreneurs. They were aligning their social purposes with the need to create sustainable models for their organisations.

These women wanted to be in charge. They didn't want to be in the back seat, and they certainly didn't want to be patted on the head and hear people saying: "You are a social entrepreneur, good on you!"

We realised that no specific forum existed at that time for women social entrepreneurs in Europe. So we stepped up to establish this space, where women from different sectors could join in a common conversation and learn from their peers, while developing their business.

I saw thousands of women going through all these years of conversations, shared experiences, public events, coaching sessions filled with tears, torn business plans and business failures. What made some more fulfilled, more efficient and more impactful than others, was the capacity to leave the economy of loneliness behind and create an economy of connectedness.

Here is what they did:

1. They gave themselves permission

Female social entrepreneurship is invariably connected with deep-scarred systemic issues such as sexism, violence, exclusion (among others). These topics are delicate and hard to create buzz around, because mainstream audiences don't like to talk about pain.

So whenever you want to raise awareness, you need to find a way to retain people's attention. Give yourself permission to be vocal. Don't allow anyone to put you down for raising important issues and find a way to make people listen to you without alienating them.

2. They designed a system, not just a product

You will see social entrepreneurs receiving praise and accolades for their work and rightly so. But what a lot of them don't grasp is how to design a system that is working for all stakeholders involved, whilst being future proof.

We need more social entrepreneurs who are system designers. People who have empathy, and are able to put themselves in the shoes of their beneficiaries, feel the bugs along the way and co-design and prototype simple solutions.

A great example is 'The Good Kitchen' – a project that designed a new food service for senior citizens in the Holstebro Municipality in Denmark. The project covered all aspects of their public food service, from users to kitchen staff and other relevant parties. Prototypes of the new design were tested with users and were iterated based on their feedback. In the end, the team was able to develop a new solution that not only led to more customers and sales of healthy meals, but also increased staff pride and job satisfaction – and a prestigious design award!

3. They thought circular

As you read this, you might think: How can I influence the world, when I feel so disconnected with the decision makers? How can one person change the dreadful news I am seeing on TV?

I suggest you to connect the dots and start to think 'circular' in everything you do.

Think of your enterprise as part of an economy that is restorative and regenerative by design; an economy that accounts for its losses and gains, not just in financial terms, but also in terms of well-being, gender equality, natural resources, transparency, and accountability.

In everything that you do, you are already influencing the world. In your social enterprise, in the consumption choices you are making at home, and also as a professional in a large corporation (should you decide to be part of the corporate world one day). What goes around comes around.

4. They knew their boundaries

I saw a few social enterprises collapse because of balance sheets that couldn't keep up with reality. People need to eat. People need love. People need connectedness. If your business doesn't feed you, you are creating more poverty. What is the point of being a social entrepreneur, if you can't sustain yourself and protect your own children from scarcity?

You will succeed, because you will know when to say 'No' at the right time. You will succeed, because you will stop blaming others for your pain and you will start taking action. You will succeed, because you will ask for help, when you can no longer make decisions, and you will decide to listen to the pieces of advice that warn you about what is to come. You will succeed, because you will take time to draw conclusions.

Social entrepreneurship is not an act of grandeur. It is the sum of everyday connections and small acts of trust and generosity. You will succeed when you can see how the world is connected and when you have realised how your small contribution can create a ripple effect, simultaneously within yourself, at home in your community and in the world.

I wish you all the best for your endeavours!

Servane

About the author:

Servane Mouazan is a French entrepreneur based in London. She is the founder and CEO of Ogunte, a social business development company under which she has created Make a Wave, the first incubator for women social entrepreneurs. Servane has worked across public, private and third sector organisations, focusing on talent development, social investment with a gender lens, system design, and social impact. She has worked across industries in Brazil, France, Holland and the UK, and sits on various social innovation organisations' advisory boards and challenge prizes. She has also set up the International Women's Social Leadership Awards - with 137 high profile finalists, from 23 countries, and 20 winners globally, and runs the Womanity Awards Programme, an initiative that invests in an ecosystem preventing violence against women through replication of innovative models and ideas.

Letter No. 25

Veronika Linardi, Founder and CEO of Lindardi Associates, Qerja.com and Jobs.id

Dear Female Founder,

My name is Veronika Linardi and I am based in Jakarta, Indonesia. My fascination with technology propelled my breakthrough beyond traditional recruitment into the online realm. In addition to Linardi Associates, an executive headhunting agency, I co-founded and serve as Chief Executive Officer to both Qerja.com, Indonesia's first online community that empowers professionals to make the best career decisions, and Jobs.id, the fastest rising and leading job portal in Indonesia.

This all might sound very impressive to you, but I can tell you it has not been an easy journey to get here. What seems to be an overnight success is indeed the result of hard work and building the business step by step.

So what advice can I share with you for your own journey?

Being a female founder is definitely a road less travelled – especially when options are aplenty; to be a home maker, professional or even the preferred lifestyle choice of a 'tai tai', spending most time taking good care of themselves, going to salons, gym, shopping and enjoying the company of other ladies of leisure.

But if you decide to spend your time a bit more productively (which I hope you do!) and carve out your legacy independently, then think about why you are doing this and what you want to achieve by going into entrepreneurship. What is your mark?

Being your own boss can be fantastic, but on many days, things are definitely looking more like a long, winding marathon than a bed of roses. For starters, in the early days, you don't have a constant stream of revenue, let alone being profitable. Can you live with that?

Tenacity and determination are very, very important. Starting a business is like giving birth to a baby. It is your full responsibility to grow and nurture it. If you are not there to feed it, it will not survive. It's as simple as that.

In case this truth hasn't scared you away yet, let me share some tips with you that will help you build your company:

Start when you are young. You'll have less baggage, less responsibilities and less financial commitments.

Always keep in mind: what doesn't kill you makes you stronger. Gathering experience through trial and error is always good. Most successful entrepreneurs have failed plenty of times before they got to where they are today.

Learn from more seasoned and experienced leaders and build good relationships with them. This will not only enable you to leapfrog all the lessons learnt, but also open up a lot of doors for you.

Go with your guts. When push comes to shove, you need to make an executive decision. Not making a decision at all is actually one of worst things you could ever do as an entrepreneur.

Invest in building a great team. Find people you can respect, who are better than you and who complement your skillset. Don't feel threatened by talent.

Make sure to vet your co-founders. You're going to have an intense relationship with them, almost like in a marriage. The exciting honeymoon period will fade and you will still need to go through thick and thin together. So think about: Can you agree to disagree? Bite the bullet for the greater good? Are your values aligned? Do you have trust and belief in that person? All very important questions...

Be clear on your targets and make sure you hit your metrics. Whatever businesses you are in, there will be a lot of numbers to abide to. Make sure your key metrics fit your business model.

What does that mean, you ask? Well, think of it in a simplistic matter: Are you working to achieve growth or profitability?

If you are looking for growth, then how fast is your user base or audience growing? How popular is your product? What is your cost per acquisition?

If you are looking for profitability, then see how many people are still buying your product when you switch from free to paid. If it's already a paid product, then how is it growing compared to your competitors? For every customer that you have, how many new customers does he or she refer to you?

All these questions and many more will await you in your startup journey. You might feel a bit overwhelmed now, but trust me, building your own business is one of the most rewarding and empowering things you can do in life.

So be brave and best of luck!

Yours,
Veronika

About the author:

Veronika Linardi is a serial entrepreneur based in Jakarta, Indonesia. She is the founder and CEO to multiple successful ventures and has built an empire in the Indonesian recruitment industry, helping hundreds of companies find the right talent and bringing transparency to jobseekers. Before deciding to tread the land of startups, Veronika has worked in the intersection of business development, strategic planning, management consulting, operation and advertising for companies like Charoen Pokphand Indonesia, CNN, Bozell Worldwide and PriceWaterhouseCoopers (USA). She has obtained a bachelor degree from University of Texas and a master's degree from Carnegie Mellon University before she turned 21 years old. Outside of work, she enjoys yoga and spending time with loved ones cooking and eating.

Letter No. 26

Nadine Sinclair, Founder and CEO of Shrewd Foods

Dear Female Founder,

My name is Nadine. I'm the founder of Shrewd Foods. Looking back on my journey as an entrepreneur, there are many things I wish I had known before starting out. Here are my top three pieces of advice that I would like to share with you for your journey.

1. Ask the Five Why's

As entrepreneurs, we encounter and solve problems every day. However, sometimes you might find yourself solving the same problem over and over again. This may be a sign that you are trying to solve a symptom of a problem, and not the underlying problem itself.

In this case, it is time to dig up the 'Five Why's' – a powerful technique developed by Toyota which will get you to understand the root cause of any problem by asking 'Why' five times.

Here is a practical example. Let's say, your problem is: "Our online sales decreased last week."

Using the 'Five Why's' technique, you could discover this:

1. Why did our online sales decrease?

Because less people placed an order.

2. Why did less people place an order?

Because customers abandon their carts during checkout.

3. Why do customers abandon their carts?

Because they do not get referred to the payment provider.

4. Why don't customers get referred to the payment provider?

Because the link is broken.

5. Why is the link broken?

Because the payment provider recently changed it.

If you had stopped at the first 'Why', you may have decided to send a special offer to your customers or you may have invested in some more online marketing. If you had stopped after the second 'Why' you may have sent an email to the customers reminding them of the items in their abandoned carts.

By following the technique, you did not only identify the root cause of the problem, which can be easily fixed, you probably also saved yourself a lot of money and avoided additional frustration for your customers.

2. Walk in your customer's shoes

You probably have heard that one before. But what does it really mean? Yes, you can picture how you would feel and what you would wish for, if you were your own customer. You can ask prospective customers what they would expect from you, and you can ask your existing customers what you can do to improve their experience with your product and your company. You should be doing all of these things, but there is more you can do.

In my experience, nothing beats literally putting on a customer's shoes. Not once, not twice, but as often as you can. Go out there and shop for a product your target group uses or buy similar products to your own. Experience and document your own decision journey.

- How do you learn that the product is out there?

- Where do you look for information?

- Which reviews do you trust and why?

- What do you look for on their website or in shops?

- What information are you missing?

- What do you really like or dislike?

- What is your first impression of the product?

- What aspects of the product shape this first impression?

- What do you really care about when using the product?

You can use almost any consumer experience you have in your life to think about what implications it has for your own product, and how you interact with your customers.

3. Trust your instinct when hiring

Hiring the right people for your startup is one of the most important things you will be doing, and one of the most difficult too. It is easy to rush hiring, simply because you urgently need someone to get the job done or to fall victim to the pedigree effect.

Just because a CV looks good on paper and the person says all the right things during an interview, does not mean that the person is bringing in the commitment and the passion you need to build a business and a great team.

Looking back at a number of hiring choices we made, there are two things I wish I had done differently: trust my instinct and make unpleasant decisions more quickly. No matter how good a CV looks and how many rational arguments there are, if your gut feeling doesn't say 'Yes', then don't hire that person. Equally, if things don't work out with your new employee, let him/her go as fast as possible. Don't try to 'fix it' or 'give it more time' or wait for him/her 'to turn things around'. Your startup has a low life expectancy to start with and your team is working at their limits to beat the odds. Make unpleasant decisions quickly as hard as that may be. You don't have resources to waste.

I hope these tips will help you save some time and heartache in your startup. I'm proud of you for embarking on this journey!

Yours,
Nadine

About the author:

Nadine Sinclair is a German food entrepreneur based in Munich. She is the founder and CEO of Shrewd Foods GmbH, which offers healthy DIY smoothies made out of 100% fruit. Even though she was born into a family of entrepreneurs, she chose to study biotechnology in the UK as well as Germany. After earning a PhD in Molecular Biology, she became a management consultant for McKinsey. After a 6-year career, she left McKinsey to finally start up her own business. Nadine has worn and continues to wear different hats in her professional life and is able to speak many languages because of that: science, consultant, business, coach, challenger and common sense.

Letter No. 27

Heidi Lindvall, Co-Founder and CEO of Storygami

Dear Female Founder,

My name is Heidi and I'm the co-founder and CEO of Storygami.

Running a startup is the most difficult thing I have ever done in my life. There are times when I doubt our idea, and there are nights when I lie awake wondering if it will ever work. I also constantly ask myself: "Am I capable of running a million dollar company?" or "Did I earn the right to be called a CEO?".

You should know that the life of a startup founder isn't glamorous. You might lose your hobbies and your weekends, and to some extent you might start to forget the person you used to be. Your friends and family might feel that you are distant and you aren't the same person you were before. They are right. You are not that same person anymore, but that's ok.

Running a tech startup is also the most rewarding thing that I have ever done in my life. I wake up every day with a purpose, knowing that we have built something that has the potential to completely change our industry for the better. I have sacrificed a lot of my time and effort for this company, but I genuinely care about the change that we are making and I am proud to be able to work on this everyday.

In the past years, since starting my first company, I have grown more than I did in the 10 previous years. While some might still not understand or agree with the choices that I have made in my life, I wouldn't do anything differently. So what are the most important things that I have learned in the past 7 years?

It all starts with the people you surround yourself with. Surround yourself with people who are smarter than you, people who have a different worldview, a different skillset and people who constantly challenge you. You will need help with both small and big questions, so you need a range of people that you can turn to with the different challenges that arise. There will be small things like "How do I set up my legal stuff?" or "How do I file taxes?" that you just need some expert advice on, but there will also be bigger things like "How do I motivate my team?", "What are the main KPIs I should be tracking?" and "What do you do when your biggest client decides to leave?". You can't be afraid to ask questions, however big or small they might seem. Sometimes your friends or mentors might have the answers you are looking for and sometimes you will notice that you have the answer yourself – you just needed to externalise your thinking and you needed a sounding board.

It is also very important that you trust the people you have surrounded yourself with, and that you believe that they have your best interests at heart. Whether it's an employee, a mentor, or a friend, don't waste your time around people who you don't trust or wouldn't be friends with outside of work. I have learned the hard way that you can't help people who refuse to step up for their own sake. If they let you down once and don't take responsibility, they will probably do it again. I have tried to give second and third chances, but have always realised that broken trust can't easily be fixed and, although it's hard, sometimes it's better just to let go.

You will also come across a lot of 'talkers' and 'wannabe mentors'. These are people who are opinionated and advise you on how you should be running your company, what attributes successful leaders have etc. without having any real life experience to back these up. Be careful with these people. They are often confident and they want to be seen and heard, so they might come across as experts and authoritative figures. They might have impressive lists of startups that they have worked with and they might be very well connected, but always question where their experience comes from. This is dangerous as we tend to want to trust people, but not everyone in business can be trusted and you will waste a lot of time taking advice from these people. Don't waste your time on people who 'talk the talk', unless they also 'walk the walk'; they might not be worth your time.

There are also people who might make you feel that you don't belong in a board room, onstage, or in your industry, simply because it's hard for them to see someone in a position of authority who doesn't look like them (a young, blonde woman, in my case). They aren't necessarily bad people, they aren't mean or intentionally sexist and they might welcome more diversity into tech. But they simply aren't used to seeing people like you running multimillion-dollar companies. Some women might feel sorry for themselves in this situation and others might try to change how they dress or present themselves just to fit in.

My advice, however, is to ensure that you are extra confident when you walk into that room. This confidence will come from knowing the answers to their questions, knowing your numbers, doing your homework, and 50% more. Being over-prepared allows you to exceed people's expectations of you and your company, and that is pretty empowering. Having to do this might feel unfair, but that is the world we live in right now, and the only way to change people's perceptions is to prove them wrong. There will be some whose minds have already been made up. Don't waste your time on them. Just move on and focus on what you are here to do.

The last point I want to make is that entrepreneurship is not for everyone. You might have a great idea, but unless you feel that you can run this company better than anyone else and that you simply need this company to exist, then you shouldn't start it. Running a company is hard enough, and unless you are 100% passionate and dedicated to what you are doing, it is not worth it.

Even if you fail (and at some point you will), you need to be able to shrug it off and be proud of the change you tried to make and what you spent all those years working on. If you can learn to be proud of what you have done, then you can't lose.

I wish you all the success on your journey!

Heidi

About the author:

Heidi Lindvall is a Finnish entrepreneur who is passionate about storytelling, video, social issues and startups. She is the co-founder and CEO of Storygami, a company that is revolutionising online video by helping video creators engage with and educate their viewers, while earning real revenue through their videos. Storygami was chosen to take part in the 500 Startups accelerator (Batch 13) and has managed to attract clients like Virgin, BT and Al-Jazeera. Heidi previously co-founded Codoc, an award-winning digital video company dedicated to creating spaces for critical thought through media. She is a Virgin Media Pioneer and a Finalist for Women of the Future Awards 2013.

Letter No. 28

Sharmadean Reid, Founder of WAH London

Dear Female Founder,

I have said many motivational things in many motivational places, but to you, dearest female founder, I am going to tell it like it is.

Well, isn't this crazy?! You want to start your own business! You have seen a gap in the market and you have found the perfect solution! YAY!

Hold up. Rewind...

This is what happened to me. I am an accidental entrepreneur. I mean, I have always been commercially minded. I took business studies from the age of 11, but up until founding WAH, I had only worked on projects for clients and had never run a customer facing business.

I definitely made a lot of mistakes and last summer I made a conscious decision to fix up. I had just been awarded my MBE, but it felt undeserved. I felt like a bit of a fraud for being held up as the poster girl of a self-made British businesswoman, when, in reality, my business was a mess and I was a mess.

I know, I know, overachievers are hard on themselves and women don't often self-praise, but deep down inside I genuinely felt that, although I had achieved a lot on a surface level, I hadn't achieved anything substantial at all.

I started thinking differently about myself and about my business. What had I done to slow our growth? What is the model that is going to truly make us stratospheric? I started slowing down on the crazy ideas that I had and speeding up on building the foundations of my company, so that my crazy ideas would actually have something to stand on. So here are a few tips I have for your journey.

Firstly, stop thinking of yourself as a small business owner and act like you are a global CEO from Day 1. Becoming a founder is the first step, and the entrepreneurial way of thinking is what will keep you innovating, but there will be a point where you will have to act like a CEO, if you want to grow your company into something serious and sustainable.

Secondly, get a co-founder or a team in place as quickly as possible. I was so used to being independent, taking care of myself, and being responsible for myself, that I assumed I also had to shoulder all the responsibility of my business by myself. I immaturely thought no one would 'get me', so I preferred to work alone. How silly I was!

Don't do that yourself. You might start as a solo founder, but the right people to work with you are out there and you will meet them by socialising in places that you both are interested in. We tend to look for co-founders in our friends and family circle, but they might be too close to you and will let you get away with too many things, because they know you well. You need fresh ideas and perspectives, and someone who will not be afraid to challenge you. You may think it's super cool to say "I did it all myself. Just me. I built this business!", but investors and advisors will think that you will struggle to grow it into a global empire (and they would be quite right).

By the way, hiring cheap labour (an assistant or 'staff') to tide you over doesn't do the job. Think about getting a C-Level person on board from the minute you have your idea. Sketch out the organisational chart of your dreams and work on filling those roles. I didn't hire seriously for 5 years because I was scared of the cash flow responsibility. But the truth is, I would have achieved more growth, if I had decided to focus on my team and investment in them rather than in a fancy website or a new logo.

Thirdly, have a strategy in a place. We were a hot brand from the start and, like I said, our actions were totally unplanned. I knew that a new type of nail salon would be a cool thing to do and I knew that it would be fun to own, but I was not prepared for changing nail culture completely and being inundated with requests from every magazine or brand to work with them. With no strategy in place, I said 'Yes' to everything. I was totally unfocused and without a framework for decision-making, I was all over the place.

I would agree to projects without thinking about my return on investment. For example, we once spent £5,000 on a party to promote a licensed product, where the maximum amount of royalties I would have earned from said product based on their manufacturing order was £3,500 (duh!). It wasn't that I was incapable of this type of thinking; it's just that I wasn't trained in it. Thinking strategically wasn't my default setting. Branding, marketing, consumer engagement, making things cool, making things pretty etc – these were my default settings. Are they yours too? Because if so, know that they will only take you so far.

Don't get me wrong, they are great skills to have. After all, lots of companies don't have those skills and lots of men don't have those skills too; but you need to support them with a strong business backbone to sustain your early successes. If you do nothing else for your business, please work on your strategic planning!

We used to split our year into 'themed' quarters based on style trends like "This Spring is all about bunnies on nails!" Nowadays, my Spring quarter is all about new product development, planning our Christmas execution and growing users on a specific channel. Doing your strategy on a timeline or roadmap allows you to foresee problems in advance rather than being surprised by them as they pop up. If you plan on doing 5 pop-up salons for summer, then you know that you need to start the hiring process to deal with the extra workload in April. Proper planning simply allows you to be prepared better for any type of challenge.

And finally, get mentors and advisors on board! If you don't come from an entrepreneurial background, never did an MBA or worked at Goldman Sachs etc., you might discover networking structures that seem weird to you. As women we don't often ask for help at the risk of being perceived as weak. For guys, this is not a problem. In fact, whole pastimes have evolved to serve the purpose of networking and mentoring (golf, anyone?).

There is no shame in asking someone older, more experienced, male or female, for his or her advice and help. In fact, most people will be completely flattered, and if they believe in your business, they will actually be the best advocates for your company and spread the word amongst others at their level. Don't choose a mentor lightly. If you want a regular person to act as your mentor or sponsor, meet them a few times socially first. See if you gel, and see if you can truly learn from them. Then, ask them outright and let them know exactly what their commitment will be. For example: "I would love you to be my mentor, can we meet a few times a year just to get your input on myself as a CEO and how I am running my business? I would really value your advice."

Decide who you want as mentors, advisors, investors, or board members, because they are all very different. I used to think that investors acted as mentors (yes, I really did!), so the minute I didn't really like them I was like "No, thank you!" What a stupid mistake!

You need to surround yourself with as many people as possible who know more than you do. Be clear about what information you are gleaning from them. One businesswoman might be amazing for insight into distribution strategy, a potential investor might be good for networking, and a former Vice President of a huge blue chip corporation might be brilliant at shaping your leadership style in order to steer your company to IPO.

The road is long and it certainly is lonely. So, think big to build something long standing, surround yourself with an amazing team to lift you up when you are tired, have a strategy and a roadmap, so you actually know where you are going, and get some advisors to act as juice bars along the road, where you can stop by every now and then to get some nourishment.

Business is no joke, but it can be so rewarding. You have taken an active decision to control your life. To me, true empowerment is economic empowerment and you have taken that first step.

Congratulations!

Shar

About the author:

Sharmadean Reid is a British entrepreneur based in London. She started her career as a stylist and brand consultant for Nike and ASOS. In 2005, she founded WAH Zine, a photocopied fanzine to connect girls in hip-hop culture together, handing it out at clubs across London. In 2008, she had an idea to create a nail salon that brought together her magazine and blog readers in one place. WAH Nails was founded in the summer of 2009 and changed nail culture (and the beauty landscape) ever since. She is now CEO of WAH London Ltd with a cult salon and a nail product line distributed globally. Sharmadean is mother to a 5-year-old boy and holds a bachelor degree in Fashion Communication from Central Saint Martins. She has been awarded a MBE for services to the Beauty Industry by HRH Queen Elizabeth.

Letter No. 29

Pearl Chan, Principal at Omidyar Technology Ventures

Dear Female Founder,

First off, I want to congratulate you on making it this far! Starting and running your own startup is a huge accomplishment – no one can ever discount the passion, energy, hard work, and time you have put into your company. I am constantly in awe and inspired by you, a talented women entrepreneur building something amazing.

I wanted to share a bit of myself with you before we dig in. I am currently an early stage investor looking at working with startups, and the very best part of my day is meeting with and being inspired by great entrepreneurs. Outside of work, I am a native of San Francisco and love a great hike or science fiction novel.

In thinking through this letter, I really thought hard about trying to put down my thoughts from the point of view of what I would want to tell my best friend if she was about to start a startup.

These are some of my thoughts in a nutshell:

Never underestimate yourself. You have got this far founding your own startup; so never, ever underestimate yourself no matter what people say. People will always try to discount you, but I am a fan of a Vince Lombardi quote that I heard at the start of my career "It's not whether you get knocked down, it's whether you get back up."

Stay true to your compass. Stay true to yourself and always keep a strong compass with regards to the mission of your business, what you are driven by, and who you are as a person. Often times I will see entrepreneurs get swayed in various directions or try to mold to fit a stereotype, but the best ones learn to get comfortable with their own style.

Go in with a prepared mind. Investors will expect you to know your business inside and out (e.g., competitors, unit economics, etc.). Always go to meetings well prepared, and stay close to your startup. Early in the life of your startup, it's important to own all strategic areas and really understand your data.

Reflect openly. Always be open to feedback, and constantly reflect and iterate in relation to both your startup and yourself. I've also found the best entrepreneurs ask lots of questions, and even if they don't end up working with an investor or advisor they always seek constructive feedback.

And finally, have fun. Working on a startup is extremely hard but an incredible journey. Life is short, so make sure you are surrounded by good team members and continue to be driven by your mission. Also, always try to carve out some time for yourself. I know work life balance can be a myth for many entrepreneurs, but even a small dinner, hike, or exercise out of the office can make a difference.

Another quote that keeps me driven by Vince Lombardi is that "The price of success is hard work, dedication to the job at hand, and the determination that whether we win or lose, we have applied the best of ourselves to the task at hand".

I have no doubt that each and every one of you will make your mark on the world (and build a kick-ass company)!

Best,
Pearl

About the author:

Pearl Chan is Principal at Omidyar Technology Ventures (OTV), a Silicon Valley-based venture capital firm where she invests in all types of disruptive internet & mobile platforms. A San Francisco native, Pearl enjoys working with passionate entrepreneurs looking to leverage technology to disrupt various market categories. Her passion for helping companies started at an early age when she saw first-hand how her father built his own business. From that point on, she was hooked on understanding how businesses succeed. She started her career at Goldman Sachs where she helped companies navigate IPOs and M&A and at Tinicum Capital where she helped evaluate investments in telecommunications and technology. Pearl graduated in Applied Mathematics and Economics at the University of California, Los Angeles. While at UCLA, she also helped build a women career-focused network.

Letter No. 30

Therése Gedda, Founder and CEO of 30minMBA

Dear Female Founder,

It was over 14 years ago, but I remember like it happened yesterday. I was sitting on the old English couch in the office of the President of Sweden, she had just stepped outside to take a quick call, and I was by myself. Sometimes in life, we experience a moment when the opportunity to fulfill our dreams appears and everything seems to fall into place. This was one of mine.

The question was still hanging in the air. "Do you want us to employ you or hire you?"

I took a sip of hot coffee and thought about how I always knew I would eventually start a company when I was older. When she opened the door, I felt the excitement bubbling inside me and said: "Hire me!". That was the day I started my first management consultancy, which I ran for over a decade. I was 17 years old at the time.

We all have moments that shape our path. Seizing this opportunity made me an entrepreneur. What made you decide to become one?

I'm Therése by the way, the Founder and CEO of 30minMBA.

First of all, welcome to the entrepreneurial lifestyle! This lifestyle is full of adventure, personal and professional growth, a strong sense of achievement and moments of brilliance. It is also one of the hardest things you can do. You will be challenged to solve problems that you didn't know you are about to have at the beginning of the day, and you will feel frustrated. But don't be discouraged – it is going to be the experience of a lifetime, filled with so many magical moments.

Over my years as a founder, keynote speaker and startup mentor, I have had the pleasure of meeting thousands of amazing people from all over the world. I have enjoyed deep conversations about the highs and the lows of entrepreneurship with passionate individuals from all walks of life. Today, I want to share 3 stories from my own journey that contain wisdom I wish I had known when I started.

1. There is no spoon

Just as in the movie The Matrix, limitations are only in your mind. There isn't one way of building a successful company or of being a founder. There isn't one magic formula.

It might be unusual to become the founder of a management consultancy at the age of 17, but in my mind, this was normal. I have never seen age as an obstacle or that you need to do things in a particular order. While studying at the Stockholm School of Economics, I was guest lecturing both there and at the Royal Institute of Technology about entrepreneurship and startups from the age of 21. I became a jury member at business plan competitions when I was 23.

Age doesn't matter; and it doesn't matter when and where you start – your entrepreneurial journey is out there for you to create. Don't get me wrong, knowledge and experience are important and you will also need to work incredibly hard, but your mindset will play a huge role in how you will perceive and feel about yourself.

Having a mindset of constant learning, seeking out the possibilities and complete dedication to your purpose will help; as will a mindset of paying-it-forward and giving back. There are so many people involved in every success. Remember to keep your supporters, champions, and entrepreneurial soulmates close and you will never be alone, even in the darkest moments.

Follow your intuition. There is no one way of achieving greatness. Don't do anything because it's cool or trendy. Create your own path in line with what you believe in and what your goals are.

Remember, there is no spoon. The only limitations that exist are in our minds.

2. Imagine your dreams as goals

I have always dreamt about driving change on a global scale together with like-minded people. Years ago, I realised that this is what had been guiding me since I was growing up. I'm passionate about empowering people to reach their full potential, and somehow most things I have done were related to this. The idea of building a company on this foundation paired with the latest technology in a growing market was exciting to me. Let me rephrase that, it kept me up all night!

30minMBA is built upon that dream – a dream to make a difference, to empower people and to bridge the gap between what science knows and what business does.

By expressing what you dream about, you will be able to develop goals around those dreams and bring them to life. Do you want to look back at your life and regret all the things you didn't do? Or do you wish to have a life full of joy and fulfillment due to your courage to pursue your deepest passions and by giving it your all?

3. Design your business culture

As mentioned before, there are many ways of building a company. The same goes for how you design the culture of your startup. It is easy to fall into the trap of the 9-to-5 routine; ignore it and build a business around a strong purpose instead. Develop your company and culture based on your values.

At 30minMBA, we have a great team spread over three continents and we believe in working when and where you are creative. So we designed a work culture optimised for when our team members feel most inspired and perform at their best. The larks work in the morning and the owls during the night.

When are you most creative? Design a company optimised for when you and your team members are at their best.

I know you have an amazing journey in front of you. Together we are changing the world, so if you need anything, feel free to reach out anytime.

Yours,
Therése

About the author:

Therése Gedda is a Swedish serial entrepreneur based in Stockholm. She is the founder and CEO of 30minMBA, a mobile learning startup which lets you develop your business skills when it fits you. Besides running the award-winning company, she is also a seasoned motivational speaker on topics including entrepreneurship, business culture, the entrepreneurial mindset and personal branding. Since 2002, Therése has supported thousands of founders, management teams and professionals in several countries to achieve great results in leadership, strategy, communication, marketing, and growth. She has also been a guest lecturer at Stockholm School of Economics and The Royal Institute of Technology, as well as a jury member at the Venture Cup business plan competition. Therése holds a masters degree from the Stockholm School of Economics and has been awarded Sweden's largest prize for innovators, SKAPA, in memory of Alfred Nobel. When she is not on stage, connecting people or running startups, she is passionate about training and motivating others as a fitness instructor.

Letter No. 31

Anna Guenther, Co-Founder and CEO of PledgeMe

Dear Female Founder,

It's 2016. I've been doing this business thing for a few years now and according to outside viewers, I'm making a good go of it. But it hasn't been easy. Even now, I occasionally look at the ads from Volunteer Service Abroad to see what 'real job' I could get, once this is all over.

Here's five bits of advice I wished I had known when I first transferred that $5,000 dollars into the company account to give the startup world a whirl in 2012.

1. Document expectations

If you are a little bit like me and like writing emails and compiling lists, then use this power to document relationship expectations. Most new business relationships start off great, but even the greatest start can lead to the lowest low sometimes, if you don't understand what you are getting into.

The lack of understanding doesn't occur just because of lack of communication. It occurs because your interpretation of words can be wildly different than the interpretation from others. That's not because you fabricate dream conversations, it's because everyone brings different perspectives and experiences to the table, which can lead to different understandings about what is lying ahead of you. And often, a lot of things are left unsaid that should have been discussed.

So write things down. Thrash them out. Ask questions. New shareholder? Get the shareholders agreement out. New team member? Draft up a job description and contract. New board member? Outline the terms. If it needs to be legally binding, get a lawyer to check it (and, if the agreement is with a lawyer, don't let them draft it).

Even then you won't cover everything, but getting things in writing can help conversations, at the time and later on – especially if it's signed, circulated, and stored properly. For all that's good in the world, freaking sign that shareholders agreement!

But only if it feels right. Trust your gut on this and don't be afraid to not enter a business relationship if it doesn't feel right.

2. Don't work with idiots

If you have even the slightest inkling that a person you are going to start working with is a douche, turn back. Don't engage. Life is too short to work with people you don't like. Let me repeat: life is too short!

If they yell at you, get out. If they treat you like a little girl, get out. If their emails come into your inbox and you don't want to open them because you're scared what they'll say, get out. If they think they're the smartest person in the room, get out. If you feel bad when you are around them, get the hell out!

You don't have to be friends with everyone, and you definitely don't need to work with everyone.

3. Be yourself

Your greatest asset is you. You can always learn new things, but don't try and change your core. If you are lacking skills, build them by growing your team. The joy of being in a startup is that you don't need to wear that corporate tie, kowtow to those government workers, or hide your light under an old bushel. Being authentic and being a bit quirky can get you a long way in entrepreneurship.

4. Don't be scared to ask questions

You might feel stupid. You might think to yourself "I'll google that later" (and then never do it). Don't. People like explaining things, and they might engage more with what you are doing, if they feel like they have something to add. Asking questions can smoke out the people that want to support you – and the ones that don't.

It's amazing what sorts of questions you can ask other entrepreneurs over a coffee or a drink. People in our space can be super supportive, especially if you have a few clear questions and you are willing to share your learnings (and coffee budget) at the same time.

5. Surround yourself with friends that care about you.

Starting up is hard. Staying up is even harder. You need friends that will be there when you stumble, listen when you have trouble, and feed you a meal when you are broke. If you try to do everything solo, you will probably break.

Build your support network with like-minded people, make friends, and you will be stronger. And, very important: don't compare your insides to other people's outsides. How you feel cannot compare to the game face other people put on for the world. So don't try.

Lastly, stop and look back every now and then. It's important to reflect on what you have achieved on your journey so far. Be proud of yourself, and start working on your next challenge!

All my best,
Anna

About the author:

Anna Guenther is an entrepreneur based in Wellington, New Zealand. She is the co-founder and 'Chief Bubble Blower' (or CEO) of PledgeMe, New Zealand's first crowdfunding platform. Anna started the platform in 2012 as part of a Master thesis for her degree in Entrepreneurship at the University of Otago. In its first three years, PledgeMe has raised over $7.5 million for over 870 diverse campaigns in New Zealand, ranging from food forests through to craft brewers. The platform has also crowdfunded capital for its own growth twice. Before starting her entrepreneurial journey, she had international career with New Zealand Trade & Enterprise, working in a number of roles in Shanghai, London, Hamburg and Los Angeles.

Letter No. 32

Sarah McVittie, Co-Founder of Dressipi

Dear Female Founder,

Over the past 5 years, I have been running a startup called Dressipi together with my co-founder Donna Kelly and our great team. During that time, Dressipi has developed exponentially as a personalisation service and we have brought a slew of major high street retailers on board as partners, which include Marks & Spencer, Arcadia Group, Shop Direct and John Lewis.

With this business and our past lives in other startups, we have learned lots about what you should and shouldn't do when trying to run and grow a business at the same time. There are so many thoughts, but here are three things I wish someone else had told me before I started my own business.

Learn to listen

You wouldn't know it from watching programmes like The Apprentice, but founders need to learn to listen. I have certainly learned that it's an important step towards ensuring you get what you want. We can only bring a new retail partner on board, secure investment or hire someone great if we first listen to what they want. Taking the time to listen means we can identify which aspect of Dressipi – whether that is our algorithm, our team or the way we personalise customer emails – excites that person most and adjust our approach accordingly.

The other thing I would say about listening is that you need to do it at the beginning and the end of the process. Listen to what customers and employees say when they join you, and sometimes even more importantly, when they leave you. Because that is how and when you learn your real lessons.

Learn to take calculated risks rather than a gamble

An entrepreneur is inherently risk-loving; we tend to fly by the seat of our pants way more than other people. So, how do you know that a gut feeling about something isn't just a knee-jerk reaction? There have been so many times when I was faced with a choice and had to ask myself that question. I am fairly reactive and emotional by nature, but I have learnt to take a step back and take some time to think through the issues more logically. It is only when you have done your homework that you are in a good position to take a calculated risk.

Donna and I spend our time ensuring that we know everything we can about the fashion retail business. That critical mass of knowledge we have amassed means that we are far more able to tell the difference between a calculated risk and a reckless gamble.

Of course it's not foolproof – nothing is – but knowledge is what you fall back on when you have to think a situation right through to the end. It gives you context and it gives you enough perspective to make a gut decision that's based on more than raw emotion.

Understand what kind of investment your business needs (and how much)

So much of the narrative around startup life is around how much money you have raised and how many people you employ – so much so that it can give you a misleading idea about what you want and need. It could be that you don't need investment right now. Raising capital is hard work and very time consuming, so make sure you have explored all other avenues first, including loans, bootstrapping and commercial partnerships.

If you do seek investment, make sure you really understand whom you are pitching to and do as much due diligence on investors as they do on you. At the early stages you need smart investors who can add real value beyond the funding. For example, do they know your space? And can they introduce you to potential clients or other important stakeholders? Also, talk to other companies they have invested in. This is a good way to ensure there are no nasty surprises around the corner.

Also, you really need to have nailed your product before you start raising large amounts of money. In the early stages, whilst you are still developing and proving the model – learn as quickly and as cheaply as you can. You take the same amount of time, but you spend a lot less money learning those all-important lessons. Once you have a product you really believe in, once you have proven some of the key metrics, then you are in a great position to raise money.

And last but not least...

More than anything else, you really have to make sure that you are enjoying what you do! That passion, vision and tenacity that comes as a result is genuinely priceless.

Good luck!

Sarah

About the author:

Sarah McVittie is a British serial entrepreneur based in London. She is currently the co-founder and co-CEO of Dressipi, a London based fashion technology startup which provides its personalisation technology to some of the UK's leading retailers. Prior to Dressipi, Sarah has co-founded Texperts, the world's first text message question answering service, which was inspired by her first job working as an analyst at an investment bank. She went on to raise £2.5 million from investors and collected a host of prizes. After 5 years, Texperts sold to its largest competitor and Sarah moved to New York to work for the acquiring company. Soon enough, she realised that she is a founder at heart, so she resigned and came back to the UK to start Dressipi in 2009 with business partner Donna Kelly.

Letter No. 33

Mirna Sanchez, Founder of 2ML

Dear Female Founder,

Are you wondering whether the path of entrepreneurship is something you should embark on? I would be a hypocrite if I didn't tell you right away that it is an insanely challenging task. But being a founder is the most rewarding thing a woman can experience in her professional life.

I would like to share some pieces of advice that have been shared with me along my journey. My experience has showed me how important it is to follow them and I wish I had known them from the very beginning. I think they are critical to anyone's success.

1. Always have a mentor

Having a mentor for your startup is essential, but not every mentor adds the same amount of value. Look for someone who is objective and not in love with the startup itself. Your startup will have different needs during different stages, so it could be a good idea to find different mentors who can help during the different stages. Look for mentors who you feel comfortable with and someone that you trust. If you struggle with this, ask for help in order to find the right one(s).

I have had different mentors throughout my life, but it was Marta Cruz with whom I found the right mentor for me. I met Marta through the mentoring programme of Vital Voices Argentina when I was selected as her mentee. The matching was really effective and we continue our mentor/mentee relationship after the programme.

2. Do it with passion

In order to convince other people that your business is a good idea, you must fully believe in it yourself. It is great to see women passionately working on their companies.

In the early stages, investors are looking for this visible passion as one of the central criteria for investment. Once you fully stand behind your value proposition, your investors will too.

3. Have a multidisciplinary team

Your team will be crucial to your success, but how can you build the best team? The most important thing to look for is that all team members are passionate and proactive. They should possess great communication skills and, above all, are willing to build the business with you in the long run.

Having a multidisciplinary team will certainly help to cover different aspects of the business. From marketing and sales to technical development and financial projections, there are a lot of things to be done. Don't try to do everything on your own. Embrace hiring new team members to pick up know-how that you don't have, or at least get feedback from different experts, if you can't afford to hire them yet.

4. Be patient and keep focus

Business develops in its own time and in different velocities. Sometimes you are in the 'race phase' where speed is required to win the first place, and sometimes you are in the 'recovery phase' where everything in the business is quiet and progress feels slow.

Slow doesn't mean you are doing something wrong though. For example, you may have arrived at a point where you need to find alignment within a group of people before you can move on – and the process to get alignment can take a lot of time. Or you are missing key information in order to take the right decision and getting that information takes time too.

Situations like these can be very frustrating, but it is really important to stay patient and focus on doing the right things. Decisions that are taken in a hasty way during the 'recovery phase' usually lead to wrong actions with unpleasant consequences.

I am a very impatient person, but being the leader of my own company has really taught me the importance of practising patience and focus. It also made me understand that not everything is under my control. The most important thing is that I'm aware of which phase I am in at the moment, and plan my actions accordingly.

5. Failure is not bad

Every time you fail, you will learn. So failing is actually a good thing!

My current company 2ML is my third startup. I loved the two previous ones, but they did not flourish for various reasons. I learned that, whenever you start again, you start stronger and now here I am: I run 2ML.

I still make mistakes and fail, but today I know that you only learn from the mistakes you make. Every time I go through a difficult period, I have to reinvent myself, and with every reinvention I gain new skills. I'm becoming a stronger founder, and a better leader.

Having a company is a stress test on your attitude against failure. I have always thought of failing as an opportunity for growth and since I am constantly looking to improve myself, I welcome failures.

These are my top five pieces of advice. But mind you, there is no cookie-cutter recipe for becoming a successful founder. Once you go out and start building your empire, you will learn what works best for you.

Ask for help, do it with passion, invest in your team, be patient, and allow for failures. If you follow these principles, you will find success, I'm sure!

All my best,
Mirna

About the author:

Mirna Sanchez is an Argentine scientist and entrepreneur, born in Buenos Aires. She has earned a PhD degree in biotechnology at the National University of Quilmes. During her studies, she was a fellow of the National Scientific and Technical Research Council (CONICET) in Argentina and won a scholarship from the Deutscher Akademischer Austauschdienst (DAAD) to carry out research in Germany for two years. After winning several startup competitions, she currently serves as the CEO of 2ML, a company focused on the development of nano-biotechnological solutions that minimises human error, reducing time and bringing simplicity to scientific experiments.

Letter No. 34

Kasia Gospos, Founder of Leaders in Heels

Dear Female Founder,

I'm Kasia Gospos, the founder of Leaders in Heels, an Australian online community, magazine and a stationery brand that aims to nurture, inspire and empower female leaders and entrepreneurs. I am also the creator of Make Your Mark leadership notebooks, and author of 'Get Your Life Back', a book about how to streamline and automate your business processes and life so that you have more time for what you really love.

As the CEO of Leaders in Heels, I get lots of opportunities to read about, meet, interview and learn from other successful female founders. I also run my own business and help young entrepreneurs get their products off the ground by promoting them in our magazine.

So here are my top tips for first time female founders:

1. Pre-sell

When I launched the Make Your Mark notebook, my first ever physical product, I decided to crowdfund, because the printing company required a volume of at least 2000 units.

Even though I would have sufficient cash to outlay the cost, the crowdfunding activity proved to be a much more valuable proposition than I had anticipated. As most of you will know, crowdfunding provides the opportunity to value the demand and minimize the risk that is inherent in any capital consuming business. But what I discovered is that it also created lots of media opportunities to talk about the product, the business and myself as well!

As PR is really expensive, having a campaign – an event – made it easier to excite journalists and have them talk about the product rather than a typical product launch. It was also a social engagement tool that helped me build a community of passionate fans who were genuinely interested in helping me succeed. They ended up providing lots of feedback and encouragement!

2. Start before you are ready

I have been asked many times about how I come up with ideas – and most importantly how I get them implemented in such a short period of time. For example, in a five-month period I designed a whole stationery line, launched a full-on marketing campaign, which led to a successful Kickstarter campaign – all while working two other jobs.

Truth be told, these ideas don't come out of the blue in a brilliant flash of inspiration. I didn't wake up with the idea of creating a notebook to develop key leadership traits, or to design it to be a hybrid product between stationary and an actual book.

The notebook was the product of running a blog for professional women for many years, which then developed into an online magazine. It grew from a competition I ran that gave me insight into the key leadership traits of female leaders. It evolved from the Manifesto – a set of values we share and promote – that came from that research. I brainstormed many ideas about how I could help women develop those traits.

That is how the notebook came about. It wasn't a moment of genius, but the product of many years of hard work, research and development. I started way before I was ready to launch anything.

3. Follow principles

A good friend of mine noticed that I use certain principles in my business, which led me to innovate and create new things quickly. She coined these twelve principles as the 'Gospos Method':

- You do not need to know everything before you start

- One thing leads to another

- The important thing is to take action

- Start by asking questions

- Curiosity is important because it leads to development and enhances what's already there

- Measure everything

- You *cannot* be afraid of change

- Failure is a pathway to discovery

- Focus on making small continuous improvements

- Focus on being productive, not busy

- Automate, automate, automate

- Keep things simple

4. You can do anything, but not everything

Most of the successful people I know became successful because of the support they received from people they knew, and collaborations with other businesses.

In its first year, the growth of Leaders in Heels was very slow. This is despite the fact that I was working around the clock. I was Chief-of-Everything! I was in charge of website development, graphic design, promotion, social media, content and interviews. I took Photoshop courses and learned how to code HTML and CSS. That's all valuable but it took so much time!

My fiancé had a serious discussion with me and asked me to close down Leaders in Heels. I was constantly busy and had almost no time for him. This is when I realised that I was seriously putting my relationship at risk. I had no choice but to give up, or bring other people on board to help me.

This was probably the first and the biggest milestone at Leaders in Heels. I started to look for women who wanted to make a difference and were passionate about the same things as I was. As I couldn't afford to pay them a salary, I inspired them, shared my vision, and we worked on a profit-split basis.

And you know what? I didn't lose control of Leaders in Heels. It actually brought some fresh air, new skills, and new perspectives. The site grew far more quickly when I started actively engaging volunteers, contributors and partners. Best of all, it freed me up and allowed me to focus on the things I really loved. I got back some balance in my life and found time for my partner (now husband)!

5. Automate, automate, automate

If you want to enjoy your life and grow your business, then automate as much as you can, delegate the things that you don't love and can't be automated, and then focus on what you really love.

You'd be surprised how many time-consuming, repetitive tasks you have in your life. These are the things bogging you down and holding you back from fully pursuing your passions, and realising your potential.

List the tasks that take the most time in your day, and see what you can automate or delegate. You can read about how I automated and streamlined my business in 'Get Your Life Back', including case studies and interviews with over 40 entrepreneurs.

Founding a business is never easy. You will experience a lot of stress, doubt, and heartache. Sometimes you will wonder how you ever thought it was a good idea. But watching your business – your passion – take shape and grow is one of the most rewarding things you will do in your life.

Life is like a pen and you have the power to draw whatever you can imagine. But the ink is limited, so make sure you use it wisely and create the life you love. Start crafting your 'brand new' from today. Forget about the past. Your future starts **now**.

All my best,
Kasia

About the author:

Kasia Gospos is the founder and publisher of Leaders in Heels, a leading Australian online community and magazine created to nurture, inspire and empower female leaders and entrepreneurs. Kasia is not only a feminist and change-maker in the gender equality space – she also loves using her experience from her corporate roles as a Commercial and Business Analyst and Management Accountant, where she weaves meaningful stories from financial, operational and online analytics. She has successfully released the 'Make Your Mark' leadership notebook, working closely with designers and publishers. She is also the author of 'Get Your Life Back', an eBook on business automation and how she – and others – have used it to reclaim their time.

Letter No. 35

Tiffany Willson, Founder and CEO of Roomhints

Dear Female Founder,

Break more plates! Breaking plates releases stress. After the plate shatters there is a magical feeling of closure and you can start afresh. The secret to startup success is perseverance and the secret to perseverance is... breaking plates.

But in all seriousness, here are 16 points of advice for every founder.

1. Start today. Yes, really. Your excuses as to why you have not started or scaled your business are mere distractions.

2. Stories are made looking backwards, not forward. Therefore, don't worry about sticking to the 'plan'. It is impossible to perfectly predict the future; and if you do stick to a 'plan', you will quickly learn not to do it anymore. You will change throughout this journey and so should your 'plan'. Remember, the only constant is change, so instead of dreading change – embrace it.

3. Don't just attend female only events or exclusively join female only groups. You will find great support from your female founder peers, but you will build real strength and power by being a part of the whole crowd.

4. Listen to advice and other people's opinions. Believe me, people will have opinions – oh so many opinions! What you should do with your life, how you should run your business, who you should hire, what you should say, where you should live, what you should wear, etc. Listen to them, because they really are just trying to 'help'. Then silence them all and make your own decisions.

5. Everyone comes from a different perspective. You are the only one who understands your perspective; therefore, you are the only one who can make the right decision for you. Also, it's easier to get over a failure when you made the decision to do it in the first place (i.e. you have no one else to blame).

6. Learn to understand your gut. Then, listen to your gut.

7. Meet lots of strangers. Constantly be pitching strangers and testing new ideas or concepts. You can learn more from strangers than from your peers.

8. Learn to think and act in the moment. We have been trained to prepare for everything in life, and to participate when you are ready. Forget that. Yes, be somewhat prepared but get comfortable with never ever being fully prepared. Because, let's face it, in startup life you can never ever be 100% prepared for what will come at you.

9. Learn to give up control. It's far easier when you don't have to control everything.

10. Stay focused. Paint the vision of your future and stay focused. A good way to do that is by being disciplined, and by disciplined I mean military disciplined.

11. Say "No". You think you should be a "Yes" person, so why not say "Yes" to everything, right? In reality, people will respect you more when you say "No". A "No" illustrates your focus.

12. Listen to and read about successful founders, but know that you can't just replicate someone else's success story. Your story will be different and you have to create it.

13. Act small, but think big. Build confidence by proving people wrong. Be stubborn. Fail often. It makes it easier to take bigger risks.

14. Don't be too serious. The magic happens during times of play. Dance!

15. Stay diversified. Never depend too heavily on one person, company or client for your success. If you want it bad enough, you will be a big success.

16. Keep breaking plates until you make it.

All my best to you,
Tiff

About the author:

Tiffany ('Tiff') Willson is a Canadian entrepreneur based in San Francisco. She is the founder and CEO of Roomhints, a mobile application that connects you to interior designers who will help you design your space. Tiff has been an entrepreneur since she was a child, selling lemonade, customer-made jewelry and many other things. She earned a biology degree from Queen's University and also graduated from Parsons, The New School of Design. She has worked in management consulting, commercial real estate and a startup, before launching her own venture, Roomhints.com in 2012. Her work has been featured in numerous media outlets, including Fox News, American Express Open and The New York Times. In her spare time you can find Tiff visiting the latest contemporary art gallery, learning a new coding language or running up and down the Embarcadero in San Francisco.

Letter No. 36

Charlotte Pearce, Founder and CEO of Inkpact and OR

Dear Female Founder,

Writing letters is my life, I mean quite literally. My business is based upon the power of personalised letters, but when I came to write this one I was overwhelmed with emotion. Not because it was hard to write or because I didn't know what to say, but because it made me go on a personal journey that I don't go on often enough.

I sit here humbled by the experiences I have had and the people I have met along the way. I have by no means 'made it' yet (whatever that means), but in my mere 24 years on this planet I can safely say that I have gone for it!

So I write this letter to you urging you to go for it too. Live life, think big and be unforgettable! Here are a few tips how to do so.

1. Focus on your attitude

"Whether you think you can or you think you can't, you're right." – Henry Ford.

The only limit to what you can achieve is you. It is not your age, gender or current situation. When something doesn't quite go to plan, or things go wrong, it is so easy to blame others – your partner, your friends, your colleagues, or the government. But the truth is: YOU choose your mindset and YOU choose what actions you take.

So next time when you stub your toe on the bed, remember it's not the bed's fault. Don't let it put you in a bad mood for the rest of the day, and don't take it out on others. Instead, own it, take accountability and go kick the day's ass!

Your mind and your attitude are the most powerful weapons you have. Stay positive, think big, and when you find yourself blaming others or making excuses remember this diagram. Live as much of your life as possible above the line.

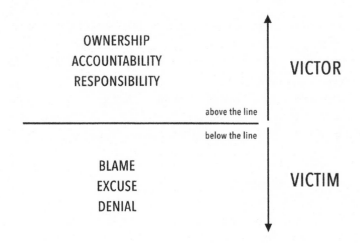

2. Ask, because no one else is

"The deepest urge in human nature is the desire to feel important." – John Dewey

This seems too simple, right? But it is rare that people ask others for help. Our inner voice says things like "Why would that person help me?", "Who am I to ask for their time?" or "Of course I can't get free office space in Central London, who would do that!".

Trust me, this inner voice is wrong. Whether you are a kid in the playground, or a successful entrepreneur, we all have an innate desire to feel important – so let's give people what they want and ask them for help!

My guess is that fear is stopping you from asking, but think about it: if a cheeky ask is the difference between landing a client or not, or between raising £1 million rather than £100.000, or between getting that free office space in Central London for 6 months for a team of 6 or not (yes, it is not impossible), what do you have to lose? Ask, because I guarantee that, more often than not, the answer will be a "Yes". Be cheeky and get that leg up. It is a great way to fast track your way to success.

3. Appreciate those around you

"Kind words can be short and easy to speak, but their echoes are truly endless." – Mother Theresa

No matter how digital the world gets, people follow people, people buy from people and people work for people. In my opinion, one trait of an entrepreneur that isn't talked about enough is their ability to appreciate and empathise with others.

We are much more likely to help and follow people who we like and trust. No one has time for a rude, self-centred business owner. Running your own business is difficult, and sometimes you feel like no one is working as hard as you, but remember not everyone is you. Appreciate the role that they play, and the small things that they do. A simple "Thank You" can go a long way!

4. Gather your A-Team

"You are the average of the 5 people you spend your time with." – Jim Rohn

Let's face it. Entrepreneurs are superheroes in their own right, and every superhero needs to gather their A-Team. Not even The Avengers could save the world on their own, so we shouldn't try to, either.

As a teenager, my dad shared with me the above-mentioned quote by Jim Rohn and I found it to be very true. We all have a friend or acquaintance who doesn't have a great attitude. They blame other people for anything and everything, nothing is ever good enough, and they hate the world. They are what I call 'mood hoovers', and there is only one place for them – out of your life!

Surround yourself with kick-ass people, people you don't mind being the average of. Reach out to those you admire, those who have tread the ground before you, and ask them for their time and mentorship. Build your support network full of awesome people, because, believe me, at some point you will hit rock bottom, and they will be there to share the times when they were there too. So, if you are going to be the average of 5 people, surely you want those 5 people to be absolute rockstars, right?

Fellow female founder, it really doesn't matter if you are 15 or 50, a data scientist or an artist, you can build the business you want, achieve your dreams and change the world. Don't let anyone tell you otherwise.

Always be unforgettable!

Charlotte

About the author:

Charlotte Pearce is a British entrepreneur based in London. Just 24 years of age, she is the founder and CEO of 2 companies (Inkpact and OR), a motivational speaker, the director of a 50k startup fund and an advisor to social enterprises. Inkpact provides software to companies that allow them to send genuinely handwritten messages to their customers with a click of a button, while supporting people from disadvantaged backgrounds. OR is a consultancy company that helps brands approach challenges in a more entrepreneurial way through working with UK's best entrepreneurs. Charlotte was described in online tech magazine Gadgette as 'a motivational machine that we have no doubt will be UK's next Richard Branson'. She was named as one of the Maserati100 in 2016 and also listed as one the 'Top 19 Young Entrepreneurs To Watch in 2016' by Startups.co.uk. She holds a bachelor degree in Management with Entrepreneurship from the University of Southampton.

Letter No. 37

Yosha Gupta, Founder and CEO of LafaLafa.com

Dear Female Founder,

You are a rare breed indeed. Welcome to the world of unicorns, cockroaches and other rare breeds! Don't worry, you are in good company.

In no particular order, here are my learnings from running my startup. My most important learning is that you will get a lot of advice from a lot of people. Ultimately, you will have to follow your gut and decide whose advice you want to trust the most. I hope some of mine might fall in that category.

Hire for resilience and commitment, not skills. All skills can be taught, but resilience only builds over a period of time. The early days of a startup are tough and you will need people who are ready to do whatever it takes. I made a lot of mistakes in my initial hiring and learnt the hard way to look for the right traits.

There will be a time in your startup lifecycle when hiring for skills will be more important, but I truly believe that resilience and commitment are the two most important traits in the early days. You are only as strong as the weakest link in your chain.

Always speak up. Yes, like most talented women I know, I suffer from the imposter syndrome too! I was so shy that I would even feel silly about writing 'CEO & Founder' under my name. I realised how many 'could you please' and smiley's I used in my emails, how much harder I would work than anyone else, always being the first one to start and last one to leave – until I finally realised what a disservice I was doing to myself.

The more you believe in yourself, the more people will believe in you. Never under sell yourself and your achievements.

Celebrate every victory. Celebrate the team's successes, even the smallest ones. It has been such a busy year for us that we have missed celebrating a lot of milestones together as a team and that has an impact on team morale – crossing 500,000 downloads in 6 months of launch, being chosen for the FB Start programme by Facebook, receiving funding from 500 Startups, further seed funding from Vectr Ventures in Hong Kong.

There has been some amazing moments for the LafaLafa team this year. All of this happened because we stuck together as a team. We hustled together and delivered together, but in our daily firefighting we forget to celebrate our milestones. So create a culture of celebrating achievements. Only a happy team can keep customers happy!

Surround yourself with the right advisors and peer group, and please make it a point to pass it on. Being a founder is hard and the only people in the world who can understand this well are other founders. Being at 500 Startups and being surrounded by other startups is what made me realise what an important support group other founders are. We all go through the same emotional pendulum and tribulations, so having people with whom you don't always have to have your game face on, who will call a spade a spade, and give you the right advice, is priceless. Be it in an accelerator or elsewhere, please go and actively seek out such friendships and build your support network. And do make it a point to pass it on, especially to other women and female founders, we all need each other.

There is no substitute for hard work. Be prepared to work the hardest you have ever worked *in your life.* I always thought I worked very hard until I became a founder. Then I understood that there is no such thing as an 'OFF' button in a startup.

And last but definitely not least, **choose the right partner** – not just in your venture, but also in your life. A large part of your life will be consumed by your startup and your partner should be the person rooting for you the loudest. I count myself blessed to have been surrounded by 'male' feminists – from my grandfather who started a university in my hometown for women where 20,000 women study every year to my father, my brother and now my husband who is my biggest critic and most vocal supporter at the same time.

My wish for you and us all is that soon this term 'female founder' will become obsolete, and that we are just founders, who are asked the same questions, who are evaluated by the same criteria and who have the same options to grow and scale their startups.

Until then, Godspeed and may the force be with you!

Yosha

About the author:

Yosha Gupta in an Indian entrepreneur based in Hong Kong. She is the founder and CEO of LafaLafa.com, India's leading mobile first coupons and cashback business. LafaLafa was selected to take part in the 500 Startups accelerator programme in 2015 and has received seed funding from Hong Kong-based venture capital firm Vectr Ventures. Before starting LafaLafa, Yosha spent 10 years in the FinTech space with her last role being a Financial Inclusion Consultant with the World Bank Group where she worked on projects across China and Southeast Asia. She also contributed to the success of Monitise, PayMate and GE Money. Yosha holds a masters degree in Finance from the Hong Kong University of Science and Technology and an Economics degree from Delhi University.

Letter No. 38

Gabriela Hersham, Co-Founder and CEO of Huckletree

Dear Female Founder,

I hope the journey is going well for you and that you occasionally manage to remember to stop, relax, breathe – and take it all in.

Sometimes it's hard for us women to do that.

My advice to you? Don't do what I did. Don't fill your mind with anxiety. 99% of the things you worry about will never happen. If they do happen, you'll deal with them then. In the meantime, focus on what *is* happening. Focus on today.

If that doesn't work, have a large glass of white wine. Life is already too stressful.

Remind yourself each and every day to see the bigger picture. There will be days where you question why you are doing what you are doing, and whether it will all be worth it in the end. Try to focus on your goals, and how you will feel once you have achieved each one. Keep your eye on the finish line. No matter what you are building, there will be days when you want to give it all up. All you can do is pray that in your next life you come back as Beyoncé.

I hate to bring up the S-word, but there will always be men who speak down to you because you are a woman. It's called misogyny, and it's their issue, not yours. Let them think you are dumber than they are. And then make them eat their hat.

That is always fun.

Always hang out with people who are smarter than you. Osmosis works. Ever played tennis against someone nowhere near as good as you – and lost? Play with the greats. That is how you get better. Apply the same rule to the people you hire and remember that growing your team is like planting a garden. The seeds you plant in your very first hires will determine what your team looks like when you are many. *Never* settle for second-best.

Always keep your costs down. My father used to go red in the face when I would agree to buy something without negotiating. He even negotiates in restaurants. I was a mortified child.

Negotiation comes naturally to people like him, but must be learned by people like me. If you are like me, find someone you can learn it from. Stalk them.

But remember that there are two areas where it pays to pay top dollar: salaries and lawyers. Find the best people. Pay them what they need to stay incentivised, and move on.

Pay your dues. At the very beginning, deem no job too small and no required task beneath you. I live at the unfortunate intersection of building workspaces and OCD. I have done some very unglamourous things. Remember the 10,000-hour rule. Becoming an expert in something takes time; so don't expect it to happen overnight. This unfortunate reality has a great way of separating the flakey from the determined.

Look around at everything you have created. You are a lucky woman.

Love,
Gaby

About the author:

Gabriela Hersham is a British entrepreneur based in London. She is the co-founder and CEO of Huckletree, a company that provides collaborative co-working offices, where ambitious minds and problem solvers come together to make things happen. A First Class Honours graduate of the European Business School (EBS) in International Business, she went on to train at the Lee Strasberg Theatre and Film Institute in New York and started her first career as an actress and producer in independent film. In 2011, Gabriela was working out of one of the very first shared office spaces in New York. Inspired by the concept, she decided to bring it back to the UK and opened the first Huckletree space in 2014. In 2015, she raised £2.4 million in Series A funding to expand the community and subsequently opened her second location in early 2016.

Letter No. 39

Vana Koutsomitis, Co-Founder and CEO of DatePlay and VinobyVana

Dear Female Founder,

I am writing to highlight five key points that I have learned in my startup journey. I will start by giving you a rundown of my experience and how I got to where I am today.

I started my career at Nomura, where I worked in Fixed Income Sales. Essentially, I was selling government bonds to central banks. I left to start my own company called The CityStreet, which is a networking company for financial professionals. I realised that finance people wanted to meet each other online and offline, but they wanted a verified network, as opposed to meeting via LinkedIn.

When I began my startup journey, I was just 23 years old. I knew it was a huge risk to leave the bank. I was giving up stability and a steady paycheck for the uncertainty of the startup world, but I knew that I wouldn't take the plunge unless I did it at a young age.

Soon after launching The CityStreet, I began dabbling in matchmaking because I realised that the people on the network wanted to date, rather than networking for professional purposes. I utilised online dating sites in order to help people find their matches. This is when I realised that there was a problem with the user experience of online dating. And I decided to go on The Apprentice competition to pitch my idea for a dating app: DatePlay, which is an application where you play games in order to meet your match.

After being on this path for over 5 years, I would like to share my 5 tips for any young women in startups or those who are planning to begin their startup journey:

Tip 1: Don't be afraid to take risks.

My first bit of advice is that you need to become comfortable with risk in order to make it in the startup world. One of the most difficult aspects of working on your own company is the amount of uncertainty involved. In my opinion, it is easier to deal with this lack of certainty at a younger age, so I always recommend pursuing your startup dream as early as possible. If you have the capacity to chase your dreams in your 20's, that is the ideal time to start your own business. Chances are, you will fail a couple of times before you hit it big, so the younger you start, the more likely you are to succeed earlier on.

Tip 2: Find a way to get your voice heard.

I chose to go on The Apprentice on BBC, because I knew that television was a great way to get my voice heard. One of the biggest issues with starting a company that relies on high volumes of users is getting those users on board and spreading the word about your project. In my opinion, this is one of the most important and crucial lessons I learnt. Even if you have an amazing product or technology, it will not grow, if you don't have a critical mass of users. I highly recommend honing in on your communication skills as early as you can, in order to spread your message effectively and broadly.

I find that women are more hesitant to speak up and have their voice heard, so this is especially important for female founders. Whether you take a public speaking course or a written communication seminar, I highly recommend that you invest in your speaking and writing skills, so that you can express yourself powerfully along your startup journey.

Tip 3: Make an impact.

I believe that, if you are chasing your passions instead of chasing money, you are much more likely to become successful in the long term. The best way for me to gauge my success is through impact. How much impact have I made and how am I paving the path for large-scale impact?

Nowadays, the word 'impact' has become a buzzword. I would encourage you to think about this and how it applies to you. How can you make an impact? How can you change the world? Think big enough to ensure that you have this wide scale effect on people and their futures. If you take this into account you are much more likely to have success in the long term.

I have noticed that women are less likely to think that they are capable of making big changes to the world and I think that is something we need to be acutely aware of. Don't let anyone tell you that you are thinking too big. The bigger you think, the more successful you will be.

Tip 4: Stay focused.

One of the biggest hurdles in my startup journey has been staying focused and on track with my plans. I highly recommend that you come up with your one, five and ten year goals and try to stick by them. If you are easily sidetracked, like me, it's easy to listen to other people's feedback and opinions and lose sight of your end goals.

If I hadn't stayed focused on my goal of connecting people, I wouldn't have gotten to where I am today. DatePlay would not exist and it would not have the traction it has, because I wouldn't have gone on Reality TV. Remember what your goals are and pursue them no matter what other people tell you to do.

Tip 5: Teach your daughters all these important tips.

One of the most important lessons for all of us is to pass our knowledge on to the next generation of women. As female founders, we are likely to encounter roadblocks that are unique to us due to our gender. Remember the hardships you have had and share those stories with your daughters and younger female family members.

Together, we have the power to change the next generation of women. We are here paving the way in order to make things easier for the younger girls, who are going to follow in our footsteps.

I hope that my advice helps you and empowers you to inspire women around you to think big, stay focused and speak up.

Very best,
Vana

About the author:

Vana Koutsomitis is a serial entrepreneur who was born and raised in Manhattan, New York, and now resides in London. From a young age, Vana has loved connecting people. She moved to London in 2009 to pursue a career in financial services. After a couple of years, Vana left to start her own networking company for financial services professionals called The CityStreet. She is now the co-founder and CEO of two companies, DatePlay, an online dating app, and VinobyVana, a brand around low-calorie, fruit flavoured wine. Born to a Colombian mother and a Greek father, Vana grew up in a multicultural environment. She speaks five languages (Spanish, Greek, French, Mandarin and English) and holds a Bachelor of Science degree from Cornell University as well as a Masters in Business Administration from Oxford University. Vana was the runner-up on season 11 of BBC 1's 'The Apprentice'.

Letter No. 40

Iru Wang, Co-Founder and Executive Vice President of MoBagel

Dear Female Founder,

I'm Iru, co-founder of MoBagel. 3 years ago, I joined the Silicon Valley startup scene, while pursuing my master's degree at Stanford University, and since then, I have registered two companies, closed one again, and raised over $1 million in investment.

People say that it takes at least 3 years in big corporations to learn something useful, but spending 3 years in the startup world? Hold on tight!

There are countless important and useful startup tips that you can find online (and in this book), but, in my experience, you can't really achieve anything without the people who back you up. And by that, I mean not only your investors and employees, but also your friends, parents, significant other etc.

So instead of 'serious' business advice, I want to share with you some practical tips (you can call them 'life hacks') around dealing with the everyday life of a startup founder.

1. Eat something at home, before going to a social dinner

The first rule for a startup founder to abide to is to stay frugal. Know that it's perfectly normal that there isn't a regular paycheck when you start out, and you have got to be comfortable with the fact that you don't make as much money as your friends in the corporate world – or any money at all.

This can lead to tough situations, especially when social events are calling. You might think of bailing out, but it's important that you still go and hang out with your friends. Eating something at home first will help you order less when you are out. Don't feel ashamed about doing this, it's a pretty common trick (however, you may keep it a secret). Every founder has to navigate through this before successfully fundraising or generating revenue. It's called ramen profitability for a reason!

2. Make time for 'dates' with your co-founders and team

Never ever underestimate people matters in your startup. Unlike in a big corporate, where the company keeps running, even if people hate each other, conflicts between startup co-founders or employees can easily make or break the entire company.

I have regular dates with my co-founders on Friday afternoon, for example. It's our sacred time, when we relax, talk about our startup, the problems we are facing or seeing at work, and life in general. Sometimes, these chats can get a bit direct or personal. That's okay, because if there are any problems between co-founders or within your team, you want to find out sooner than later.

3. Don't be afraid to be meticulous with your team

We as women tend to look closely after things – whether it's people, products, or project budgets. We can be very meticulous in our ways, wanting to know everything, and making sure everything and everyone is okay. If you are anything like that, then you might be afraid to come across as nosy or fussy.

But here is the thing: One of our investors personally told me that among all his portfolio companies, those with a female co-founder survived twice as long as those with no woman on the founding team. Why is that? Because the companies with a female co-founder got their stuff together in a more coherent way.

So don't worry about what other people think, when you are asking too many questions (again). Being meticulous is actually good for your startup. It will make you survive for longer, and you know what the most important thing for early stage startups is?

Staying alive.

4. Use some tactics to manage your mom's, dad's or other people's expectations

Next time, when your parents are giving you this worrying look and start a discussion on why you are not working for a big company, like your siblings or any other normal person, try to employ some delaying tactics. Don't brush them off, because that would be quite hurtful. A good tactic is something like "I'm going to try this startup for two years. If it doesn't work out, I still have the chance to join Google."

For me, this has worked like a charm. You save the time to explain and argue why you are doing your startup, and they save the energy worrying about you and your future. One big happy ending!

5. Treat your significant other like your investor

I know this might sound a bit creepy, but why not generate weekly reports for your significant other? In a way, he/she is investing in you with love, time, and other resources. This person deserves to know what you are up to as much a real investor. You might not see the point right now (especially when they are not in the startup space and you think that they might not 'get' what you are talking about), but you will do yourself a big favor in taking him/her along for the ride, as he/she will be able to empathize better with your successes as well as your failures.

Just like some investors, who would invest multiple times in one serial entrepreneur (even if every startup that he has done before failed), your significant other will be there to support you and cheer you up when no one else is.

These are my day-to-day tips for you, and I hope they are useful. The last thing I wanted to say is that, as far as I can see, being a male founder is just as hard as being a female founder. There is just never enough time and resources available to do everything you want to do. Therefore, I will leave you with one simple trick to manage your time and productivity: When you wake up every day, think of two things that you must get done today and focus on getting those done first. Anything additional is a plus.

A startup's goal is to stay alive until the moment when you find product/ market fit. I'm sure that this moment will happen to you eventually, but until then, don't stop believing!

Best,
Iru

About the author:

Iru Wang is a Taiwanese entrepreneur based in San Francisco. She is the co-founder and the executive vice president of MoBagel, a technology startup that provides business intelligence for IoT companies, helping them understand how customers are using their products and how they can to grow their IoT business. The company is proud to have blue chip companies such as SoftBank, Panasonic, and Philips Lighting amongst their clients. Iru began her journey as an entrepreneur in 2013, when she founded Orrzs. In 2014, she moved on to co-found MoBagel, where she focuses on fundraising, global sales and marketing. Under her leadership, MoBagel won 1st Prize at Plug and Play IoT Expo in 2015 and was named Top 5 at Slush Asia 2016. Iru holds a bachelor degree from National Taiwan University and a master's degree from Stanford University, both in Electrical Engineering.

Letter No. 41

Hanna Aase, Founder of Wonderloop

Dear Female Founder,

The first question you should ask yourself is 'Why?'. Why do you want to start your own company?

In the startup world, it is about survival of the fittest. At any given day you risk failing, but rest assured you will never lose, as the experience you gain will enrich your life. It may not enrich your bank account, but the best entrepreneurs rarely start off by caring about their finances in the first place. Having a strong 'Why' is what will make you pull through and keep you going when you feel like the opposite.

Know your 'Why'

Make sure your wish to be an entrepreneur is not just an escape from daily life. We all daydream. We all imagine what life could be like and what we could do. Wanting to start something as an escape from daily life won't be enough. Find deep purpose in what you want to build. Talk to people that would use your product.

Do you feel that your hard work becomes meaningful when you see them using your product and you know that you are adding something to their lives? If yes, then you're on to something that is worth starting and worth fighting for. I won't hide that things will be harder as a female founder. You can still do it. Just make sure to have a deep 'Why'.

For me, it all started in my early childhood when I was listening to Oprah's voice on TV: "Find meaning in your life". I knew back then that I wanted to develop something that connected us more closely to each other as people. So whenever I feel like living the comfortable life instead and give up on my dreams, I recall Oprah's voice from my childhood knowing there was meaning behind my path in life that led to what I do now.

Conquer your fears

If you are scared of starting your own company then I'm not sure you should. I know that a lot of people would say "Go ahead and do it anyway!", but here's the thing: if you are scared of starting, how will you deal with the scary decisions you will have to make on a daily basis? As an entrepreneur, you must not dwell on the idea of failure.

But what is fear really? Maybe it's just a voice inside your own head, trying to intimidate you. Do you really want to listen to it? You must believe that you *can* build this business, even if you might not know exactly how.

Make sacrifices

Starting something new usually means sacrificing something else. Sometimes it's sacrificing things you used to love or saw as a priority. You might give up on your weekends that used to be a work-free zone, or the nightly get-togethers with your friends that you used to love so much. Just so you know, I gave up shopping for 2 years when I started Wonderloop.

Habits are hard to break. Showing that you can break them is, in many ways, the first test as an entrepreneur. Read the book 'Power of Habits' and you will realise how our habits define our daily lives, our decisions and also how you will run your company.

Product growth vs. company growth

There is a difference between product growth and company growth, and it's easy to get stuck in between.

I sometimes miss the early days of Wonderloop when it was just me wireframing and working closely with the developers on an MVP. Once you are past that stage, you will need to build a team to grow the product. Your job shifts to fundraising, creating heavy materials of documentation, dealing with accounting, taxation and other 'fun' stuff.

All of a sudden, your product isn't growing anymore, because you can't remember the last time you had time to focus on it. Know this stage will come and plan for it as much as you can. This is the *limbo stage* where not being a solo founder can save you, and being one can kill you.

With Wonderloop, things grew to a point where being on my own wasn't enough anymore. The money I got from angel investors didn't allow me to hire more people. I needed a seed round to grow beyond me pulling all the weight in the company by myself.

So my advice to you: try to avoid being a solo founder from the start. But if you start alone, at least have your eyes open for co-founders as you go along the way.

Don't be too picky about your investors

Getting a high-profile investor might be important, when you are raising millions of dollars. But in the early days, spending too much time on 'who do I want as investors' will not be worth it. 99% of entrepreneurs are lucky to even get one.

So focus on what makes the company attractive to them and don't get too hung up on who they are. An exception is, of course, when you dislike the person. You don't want to be working long hours and making money for someone you don't like.

In some of the hardest times at Wonderloop, thinking of my investors made me want to work even harder, because I knew how great they were. I believe that having good-hearted people on board is more important than who they are or what qualifications they have.

Find the right people and invest in a few, strong relationships

When I started Wonderloop I knew the industry of consumer technology extremely well. It had been my previous independent consultancy job, but I didn't have the practical knowledge of how to build a tech company.

I went to conferences to get a better idea. Conferences are a great way to learn about how to get started. However, they are not always the best way to connect with people who have a lot of experience in the industry that you'd like to startup in. Oftentimes, these people have stopped going to conferences and you might have to seek them out in different ways.

After lots of networking in the beginning, I started to become more focused. Find experts in your field and dare to have them get to know you for who you are. When building relationships, invest in a few rather than focusing on everyone around you. Yes, this includes no longer checking Facebook 30 times a day.

I wish you the very best. We need you. The world and especially the investors in it are not used to female founders, which makes things harder, but is also a bigger reason to do it.

A lot of the tips above come from my own mistakes, so know that making them is just part of being an entrepreneur. Remember to grow yourself along with the company. Your company will thank you for it on the way.

Yours,
Hanna

About the author:

Hanna Aase is a Norwegian entrepreneur who is revolutionising social networking by creating the world's first video-profile identity platform. She started her company Wonderloop after being inspired by Oprah's mission of connecting and giving, and wanted to bring this to the mobile space. Her goal is to give everyone the power to be presented with opportunities and meet life-changing people with a click of a button. She believes that "If we can see everyone in the world, we could also give to everyone in the world". Wonderloop was selected as a 'Top 30 Start-Up' in the Nordics, and received a grant from the Norwegian Government in 2014. Hanna and her team now work from San Francisco and her technology has been featured in Forbes, Wired, TechCrunch, and USA Today.

Letter No. 42

Pocket Sun, Founder of SoGal and Founding Partner at SoGal Ventures

Dear Female Founder,

As a 24-year-old fellow female entrepreneur and venture capitalist, I would like to share 8 rules, or rather, 8 pieces of wisdom that I have picked up along the way. They are not rocket science, but can be transformational for your journey. Come back to visit these rules often, and reflect on how you are doing on each one of them.

Ready? Now let's begin.

1. The fact that you are here is 50% of the battle.

I believe that 90% of people are risk averse. By nature, people like things to stay the same and are uncomfortable with changes. Therefore, when you take actions to innovate, you are already way ahead of most people in the world. Remember this and remind yourself daily that what you are doing is really awesome. There will be many times, when you will feel down and questioning yourself. But despite the pain, you will realise that being an entrepreneur is the most fulfilling way to live your life!

2. Start early, or start now.

The best time to plant a tree is 25 years ago. The next best time is now. I am 24, and I wish I had started sooner. You could have become a serial entrepreneur before you graduate from college! The younger you are, the less burden you have. You are not dragged down by your family and kids, or at least not as much as you would be 10 years from now. I used to think that entrepreneurship was only something for 30-somethings, but I was so wrong. Don't wait till you are 100% ready, because you never will be! There is no quicker way to chase your dream than to start now.

3. Be a problem solver.

Acquiring an entrepreneurial mindset will make a fundamental difference in your life. It's not just about creating something cool, it's about finding pain points and solving problems. When you start looking at the world this way, you will find numerous opportunities to make a difference. Don't take anything for granted. Instead, think how things can be better. Sometimes, the problem is so obvious but no one is taking the responsibility. It doesn't mean that things should be that way. If you are suffering, it's your problem. Why not do something about it?

4. Nothing is impossible.

Nowadays, you can write, speak up, and be heard. You can almost connect with anyone on social media. You can make anything happen. Oftentimes, people will stand in your way and tell you something can't be done. Remember that all they are saying is that *they* don't know how to get it done – but they are not you! They don't know what you are capable of, and they may not understand your motivation. If no one has done it before, isn't that the best reason to do it?

5. Be a relentless executor.

Many people work for a large organisation because they like the big name. The company brand can serve as a validation of your capability and backs you as a desirable business partner. As an entrepreneur, you won't have any of that. No one knows who you are and what you do. Why would someone work with you?

As stated in Rule 1, people dislike changes, so you have to hustle and work your butt off to convince people. The good news is, this is the best experience you can get to fuel your personal growth. Just imagine, if you can get strangers to trust your little-known company and do business with you, what else could stop you from achieving your goals? I often tell people that ideas are worth nothing, because execution is what really matters. Dream fearlessly, and execute relentlessly.

6. Think bigger. Think tougher problems to solve.

Many people associate female founders with fashion, beauty, and e-commerce startups. Sure, we can be more knowledgeable in these fields, but don't limit your potential to them. At SoGal Ventures, we encourage and challenge women founders to think bigger. There are tougher problems to solve and larger purposes to pursue.

We don't invest in algorithms that can make people buy more things. We invest in technologies that improve the quality of life, create equal opportunities on a global level, and generate a positive impact on the world. Don't just start a tech startup. Rather, think deep and hard about a mission that fits your expertise and passion, and that you can imagine yourself doing in the long term.

7. Don't be afraid to be different.

I grew up in China, where I was told to do what others do and go with the flow. This mindset is toxic! It made me too quiet in team meetings, too fearful to present in front of people, and too worried about whether I can fit in. I wasted probably too much time wondering if I was 'doing the right thing' or conforming to the norm. My lesson is: It is totally okay to be different.

Even if everyone wants to build a unicorn company, you don't have to. In my case, even if everything suggests that one needs to be a lot older and sophisticated to be a venture capitalist, I decided to be a self-made venture capitalist and co-found my own VC firm. If you worry too much about following the industry standard, how can you innovate? As an entrepreneur, you get to create your own rules, stand out and kindly ignore other people's playbook.

8. Be the crazy one.

As investors, there is no one we would rather meet than someone's authentic self. You don't need to look like anyone else to succeed. One big lesson I learned early on is to know my value. If you think you're not experienced, old or good enough to bring anything valuable to the table, you are wrong. We all have different backgrounds and life experiences which can translate into unique perspectives.

Use your grit, energy, and perseverance to keep growing, but never underestimate yourself. For example, I may not have years of investment experience, but as a young millennial, I understand our generation and the current technologies better than anyone else. I may not have millions of dollars in capital, but I can provide value in different ways and add diversity to any startup's cap table through the SoGal global network. People call us mavericks because they are just not seeing where the future is. Let's be the crazy ones and challenge the status quo.

This is our era!

With love,
Pocket

About the author:

Pocket Sun is the founding partner of SoGal Ventures, the first female-led millennial venture capital firm investing in diverse founders in US and Asia. Previously, she founded SoGal, a fast-growing global community of diverse entrepreneurs and investors, where she developed and scaled a series of entrepreneurship conferences and events in multiple countries, all while studying for her masters degree in entrepreneurship and innovation at the University of Southern California. Pocket is just in her mid-twenties, but she has already invested in a dozen of startups. She was featured on the cover of Forbes Asia March 2016 issue as a Forbes 30 Under 30 Asia in Finance & VC. She was also recognised as LinkedIn 2015 Top Voices in VC & Entrepreneurship. Although her current home base is Singapore, she travels to speak at technology and venture conferences across the world.

Letter No. 43

Helene Panzarino, Entrepreneur, Mentor and Advisor to Startups

Dear Female Founder,

As a young woman in business, I never planned much. I had very short-term goals, which I would achieve, then felt some sort of lack of direction, not having planned the next step of my path.

I would reach out to people in a last minute and haphazard fashion. I never felt like I was in the right place at the right time. I remained this way until I spotted an opportunity that made me start my second business (note: I set up and sold my first business with no real plan), which forced me into planning, and it was one of the best things that could have happened to my business career.

I saw the writing on the wall – literally – in the figures that spelled doom and gloom in the business I was working in, and in a sliding doors moment, I went next door and managed to convince management to give me the client list. I won my first customers and bought the equipment that I needed to start a language training business. It was a fantastic move, and I had a great start.

What I didn't have was staff, premises, money beyond my small savings, and a destination for this cunning plan to end up at. All of these had to be put in place very quickly, with paper and pencil and a lot of legwork – but I did it. In doing this strange thing called planning, I also realised that my business targeted a niche in the market that everyone else ignored.

Was I crazy? Why wasn't anyone else seeing what I saw? Should I change direction or stick with it?

I stuck with it.

I wasn't put off by the doubters, and a few years later when I needed more space, more staff, more money and more sanity, my 'maverick' decision to focus on a part of the market others ignored, proved to be good. The political and economic landscape had changed, and I grew my business by acquiring a competitor – instant empire, secure premises, and people.

What I didn't realise is that I had created a desirable commodity and suddenly everyone wanted to buy my business. I jumped for joy, until I realised that I didn't really know how to sell a business of this size; I needed to know if I was going to get the best price and terms. I hadn't prepared for this part of the journey, even though I knew I had something special.

I hit the phones and rang everyone I knew who worked in corporate finance, investment banking, accountancy, and no one offered up anything useful. Their knowledge was for the wrong size and types of businesses – not suitable for my need.

The answer to my dilemma came in the form of another female founder who was also selling her business and who introduced me to her (fee-charging) advisers, which I can never thank her enough for.

I paid to get good advice and help with negotiating a deal, and I'm still glad that I did. When things are important, you need to do what you need to do and not rely on the free time and goodwill of others.

Anticipate where your business might possibly end up, and start cultivating relationships with the professionals you will need later on. Do your research. Meet people and have conversations. Speak to their former clients. Compare prices. Don't rely on your friends, family and networks. They may come to your rescue, but they probably won't. Suck it up and get the best deal you can, whether you're buying, selling or merging. It is all part of the process, and you will thank yourself later on.

My parting advice for you: It's not where you start, it's where you finish – or more precisely, you need to think about where you might finish when you start!

Helene

About the author:

Helene Panzarino is a serial entrepreneur, educator, mentor and advisor with nearly 20 years of experience helping SMEs and startups understand, prepare for, and access traditional and alternative funding options at all stages in their business growth. Born in the US, of German and Italian heritage, Helene has spent most of her professional life working in London, UK. She is the recent author of 'Business Funding for Dummies' (Wiley), Jan 2016 and balances her finance work life with teaching fitness classes, as well as being a brand ambassador for health and beauty brands on shopping television. A frequent round table participant, media guest and speaker, Helene combines hands-on experience with theoretical know-how. She has been nominated for the Maserati 100 Award, Prowess Award for Inspiring Women in Business, ITV Woman of the Year, and to carry the Olympic Torch.

Letter No. 44

Kelly Keenan Trumpbour, Founder of See Jane Invest

Dear Female Founder,

Do you want to know what I'm really thinking when you pitch me?

Every time you pitch, whether or not I invest in you, I admire you.

You must have done some deep soul searching just to get comfortable putting your heart, dreams and savings into a company. I see the courage it takes to stand in front of people you don't know, who control access to financial resources and networks you don't have, and ask them to flat out back you.

I also see your creativity. Female founders like you are helping the marketplace evolve in the best of ways. You tend to build businesses that are not just about solid products, but attempt to solve real problems. When you recruit teams, you have a knack for driving them to succeed while treating them like family.

If you have been in and out of meetings filled with investors who were mostly older white guys, I hope my presence gives you a moment of relief and encouragement. I know what it took for you just to get in front of me.

My job is to be selective, your job is to bet on yourself.

As much as I admire you, I'm not your aunt. You are not running a charity. I don't invest my money to say 'Atta girl'. If I invest my money, it's because you have done your job of convincing me that my resources are in better hands with you than anywhere else. If neither of us believe that, writing you a check is insulting.

Which leads me to my first piece of advice…

1. Believe that your company is the best place for me to park my money for the better part of a decade. Did your shoulders sag a little in defeat, thinking of how to go about showing me that your idea is the better custodian of my money than all other options? Because hell, how are you going to beat out savings accounts, the stock market, or all the other big companies pitching me?

Stop. That is not what I asked for. All I really asked you to do was to convince me to believe in your company – the way you believe in your company.

If you want to grow a business that attracts investors, then you need to…

2. Get comfortable trusting what you know over what you can prove to others. If you are reading this book, I'm going to guess that you are damn good at proving things. If you are like me, stuff like high grades on transcripts, degrees earned, marathons run, and foreign languages mastered give a satisfying buzz. Because who doesn't enjoy a good 'ta-dah!' moment? And not that this is ever likely to happen, but should some rude person march up to you and say "I don't really believe you can speak French", you will eloquently respond *"vous allez sauter dans un lac"*.

But in the startup world, there will be long stretches where you can't prove anything. You won't be able to prove you have a billion dollar idea until you actually have a billion dollar company. There will be many moments when your only defense will be a good game face.

That goes for investors as well as founders. How do I prove to my colleagues that they should join me in putting their money into your company? I can't and I don't. Mostly, I'm going on my intuition. It's been shaped by years of interacting with startups, multiple advanced degrees, and staying current with trends in my industry – so we are not talking about reading tea leaves here. But once I have made the call, all I can do is stand behind it and see it through. I won't know if I was right for years, and neither will you.

Once you have that gut level trust of the course you are charting...

3. Master the basics. If you are after my investment, you absolutely have to articulate four things:

1. Show me your business will grow exponentially (scalability).
2. Make me believe you and your team can deliver in an intensely competitive environment (execution).
3. Tell me about your competition and why their existence doesn't change your success trajectory (market awareness).
4. Articulate a plan for getting my money back to me with significant growth (exit strategy).

If you can't demonstrate a game plan for any one of these four things, your pitch will flame out. Again, the goal is not to prove to me that they will happen (because you just won't be able to do that). The goal is to show me what leads you to believe that they will happen.

Now all you need is to find some investors, right?

4. Don't wait to meet investors when you are raising capital. Mingle a bit in the early days of your company. Even if you don't know what you are doing, just get familiar with your local startup scene and learn more about who is who. Great places to hang out include startup incubators, universities, and demo days.

5. Have more than one approach strategy. Should you come face to face with an investor, give them a chance to know who you are before you dive into business speak. Some investors want an elevator pitch right off the bat, but most (like me) do not. Getting cold pitched by entrepreneurs is a little like getting hit on at a bar. Too much, too soon and it's in my best interest to drop the conversation.

6. Don't get offended or discouraged if an investor doesn't seem interested. If I didn't say "No" more often than I say "Yes", even to coffee dates or a quick phone call, I couldn't breathe in this industry and my portfolio would suffer. If you can't get an investor to give you the time of day, try to see that they are being respectful of your time as much as their own. Move on from that person and try new waters.

7. Find your faith. Whatever faith means to you, whichever voice you depend on to know when to persevere and when to quit, lean on it.

If you decide to keep marching on, take this with you: there are other investors like me opening doors and writing checks so that one day you can be successful enough to join us at the table.

Then it will be your turn to give a welcoming nod when a woman is brave enough to ask you to bet on her.

Yours,
Kelly

About the author:

Kelly Keenan Trumpbour invests in early stage companies and helps business owners understand what it takes to grow an idea into a business that investors will consider. Her portfolio company, See Jane Invest, has exclusively backed extraordinary women entrepreneurs. Kelly co-executive produced the documentary, She Started It, about female founders in Silicon Valley, New York, Paris and the Philippines. She has appeared on CNBC and Fox Business News, been featured in Fast Company, TechCrunch, Huffington Post and The Baltimore Sun, and been an invited speaker at Cornell, Johns Hopkins, Brown University, and University of California Berkley. She is the founding venture partner of Baltimore's NextGen Ventures and a board member of the Baltimore Angels.

Part 3
REFLECT

"Stop. Look. Listen to your heart."

Marvin Gaye & Diana Ross

Letter No. 45

Irra Ariella Khi, Co-Founder and CEO of Vchain Technology

Dear Female Founder,

What would you do, if you were not afraid? I believe that courage is gender neutral, and that it is the only thing standing between you and your goals. What if you truly believed that playing small doesn't serve the world? And that success on your own terms can – and should be – earned?

I mean what I say. Here is how these beliefs have played out for me, so far.

In the middle of London's Mayfair, I entered a dark room. All of the girls were skinny – they wore high heels, tiny skirts and tight red corsets. The establishment was seductive yet intimidating. My phone beeped. Text from my (male) friend: "Good luck with that job".

Only I wasn't there to sell my looks. I was about to pitch the owner advanced security software. My confidence grew as we talked. We bonded over interests in tech and having similar aged kids. I felt respected as a mum, a businesswoman, and a scientist. But it wasn't always like that.

Waiting with my laptop in hand, I remembered how recently I was judged in the same way as those girls in red corsets. For a decade, my entire value as a woman was based on my looks. As a professional fashion model, I quickly learned to grow thick skin. A casting agent once looked at my Model Card, circled my hip size in red, put an 'X' on it, and shouted "Send me another with a smaller ass". On average, it took 10 castings to book one job. Eventually I learned to work with it. Putting ego aside now helps me as a founder. Back then I wondered: how could you possibly 'not take it personally' when it is your face or body that is being rejected?

I lost my body when I got pregnant at 26 – and with it, my exciting career ended. A newborn baby isn't compatible with weekly travel, long photo shoots or crazy nights in the fashion world. I was a full-time mum, unemployed, resenting the routine. I was impatient, I lost perspective. I forgot to be kind; both to myself and to people around me.

I was determined to become a founder, while my partner pressed for me to 'get a normal job'. His family then strongly suggested we have another child. A plan to move countries with me as a dependant and with no work permit was made. I would be a '+1' for life, but wanted to keep working on my inventions and ideas. Everyone asked: "Not moving, no second baby, and instead you want what?". I didn't want to be a '+1'.

My family fell apart. Two years after my daughter was born, I was still an unemployed mum. Now I was also single – and homeless. I scraped together my savings and got a tiny apartment. For the next few months, I slept on a single mattress next to my daughter. I had, quite literally, 'hit the floor'.

I managed to keep working, but wish I had been better at asking for help. I wish I had been more open with my friends and family. I was too proud and beyond stubborn. I wanted immediate results, when success isn't linear or overnight. I felt stuck. Then one night, I read JK Rowling saying "Rock bottom became the solid foundation on which I built my future". I figured, if she can make it as a single mum, so can I.

Being a founder is a proactive choice, not a convenience. Like having kids, there's never a right moment to start. My main problem was time: I was always tired, juggling too much, getting nowhere. Reading "Getting Things Done" by David Allen really helped. I stressed less, and became more efficient. I also stopped saying "I don't have time" and started saying "Right now, this isn't a priority".

I wish I had been honest with myself about the importance of focus, and stuck to 1-2 things, rather than several at once. Multi-tasking is a myth; there is no substitute for dedication.

I work to be the best mum I can be, and to build a business that offers true value to humanity. No more.

Both are two sides of one coin: leaving a worthwhile legacy. For as long as I can remember, I've been obsessed with mortality. This heightened awareness that 'some day, this will all end' is liberating, and motivates constant experiments. When people ask "Why take this risk?" or "Aren't you afraid?", I remember that in the end, nothing matters. So it's ok.

I'm also learning to ask for help, and to take it. Learning that effort trumps being smart – and practicing that. In the last 6 months my company has finally taken off. Yet success comes with a price. I often feel isolated as a founder. Bootstrapping my company and lifestyle can be challenging. And I become less likeable the moment I'm successful – just because I'm a woman. Don't believe me? Look up the Heidi/Howard Syndrome.

The way I deal with this is by calling out unhelpful attitudes. It is still a man's world in the boardroom, so I practice 'The Ten Words': "Stop interrupting me. (1-3) I just said that. (4-7) No explanation needed. (8-10)". It's effective, even if I know that I'm not liked for it. In "Lean

In", Sheryl Sandberg hopes 'to be liked for her accomplishments' – I'm skeptical, but I share her hope.

So, why is being a founder worthwhile? It satisfies my drive to put my capabilities and character in service to a greater cause, because I know I *can*. And in doing so, I can make the world better. I get to invent unbelievable technology with people I choose (and who also choose me). We choose our work, clients, and life balance. And having that choice is true freedom.

"What do you want people to say at your funeral?" asked Steven Covey in "7 Habits". Here is what I would hope for: "She was a fearless but kind human being. She made society better and safer through her work, and raised a loving daughter, who learned from her mum's mistakes."

Until that day, I will keep on working. Both on myself and my legacy. Some days I'm better at being kind, other days I forget. I still aim for too much, get impatient and often feel stuck. But I keep on going, not being a '+1', and building my vision. After all, you can't fail if you don't give up. Live on your own terms. Don't die before you have to: www.paulgraham. com/die.html.

Thank you for reading.

Irra Ariella

About the author:

Irra Ariella Khi is a serial entrepreneur based in London, who is obsessed with cyber security and data privacy. She is the co-founder and CEO of Vchain Technology, a deep tech company that is developing a patent-pending blockchain solution to reinvent verification, privacy and trust. Irra grew up across Europe and the Far East, learning 9 languages, and graduating from Oxford University with a 1st Class Honours Degree. Her first career was in fashion modelling since the age of 14, notably working for brands like Guess, L'Oreal and Tom Ford. During her modelling career, she launched Soul of Fashion Media, a digital platform for up and coming fashion designers. Later on, she was headhunted to become co-founder and product evangelist for the IceCream app, before leaving to research interests in Physics and Computer Science, which lead her to create Vchain Technology. In her spare time, Irra is a speaker and mentor at Oxford Entrepreneurs, StartUpBootcamp, Said Business School and General Assembly.

Letter No. 46

Alice Bentinck, Co-Founder and COO of Entrepreneur First

Dear Female Founder,

Everyone I spoke to wanted me to take the job at Google – "Think of the free food!" Google is one of the most impressive companies in the world, but for me, I knew it wasn't what I wanted.

I was, and still am, very ambitious. I like working really hard and know that, whatever job I do, I'm happy for it to take up the majority of my waking hours. Building a startup was a way for me to do both getting the satisfaction of building something from scratch and solving a problem I really cared about.

But instead of starting a startup, I looked for a job.

Why?

1. It felt risky because startups fail. If you say you are going to build a startup, most people's response is that 90% of startups fail.

2. It felt risky to leave a prestigious company. It gave me social approval – both from my peers and potential employers.

3. It felt risky to turn down the job I had just been offered. And my peers kept on telling me how lucky I was and how excited they were for me.

But these are terrible reasons not to start a startup, as I kept thinking:

1. If 10% succeed, then you should back yourself to be in that 10%. You don't have to be in the 90%.

2. Why would you let other people's standards and choices dictate your life and career?

3. I wasn't excited by the job at Google. I wanted to build a startup, so why would I invest time doing anything other than that?

That was four and a half years ago. I am now a co-founder of Entrepreneur First (EF) where we support the world's most ambitious individuals to build their own tech startups. My co-founder and I have raised more than $15m, created 75 companies and have just opened our first international office in Singapore.

I can't imagine doing anything else with my time. It may take 10, 20 or 30 years to build EF into the institution we want it to become, but I want to spend my career focusing on that. We are changing the way the most ambitious people see their career paths and challenging the status quo of company creation. There is nothing I would rather do.

I want to see more talented individuals take the leap into founding their own startup. Here are some of the lessons I have learnt, from my experience and from helping 250 people start their own companies from scratch.

Most people won't.

Most people won't start their own startup. There will always be a list of reasons why now isn't the right time to start a startup. That list will never get shorter.

Common reasons I hear are "I haven't found the perfect idea", "I have an idea, but I'm not sure if the business model will work", "I can't find a co-founder", "I don't have a big enough network" and "I need to build more skills and then I'll be ready".

The only way to solve all of these problems is to get started. To make the leap and learn.

One of my favourite books, Mindset by Carole Dweck, has now become a mantra for EF. The book focuses on our how open we are to learning and embracing learning. Failure is fundamental for founders to succeed.

"I don't divide the world into the weak and the strong, or the successes or failures... I divide it into the learners and non learners." – Benjamin Barber

As a startup founder, you aren't expected to have all the answers. You are expected to go through the process of learning what the answers should be. Building a startup is a process of discovery and iteration. You will make mistakes along the way, but as long as you are learning and improving based on what you have learnt, you will be heading in the right direction. You can't learn to be a founder while stuck in a corporate job, in the same way you can't learn the piano by reading books.

If you look at the original idea for EF, then you would say that we have failed. It was the wrong business model. It wasn't a perfect idea. But I would never have been able to get to the right business model, or right idea, without actually working on it. It was only through trying to get people to part with their money and failing, that we learnt we needed a new approach.

Focus on your edge.

There is an opportunity cost to the startup you build: it's the other startup you could be building. A simple way to ensure that you are building the most valuable startup possible is to leverage the skills and knowledge you already have.

Your edge are the skills and knowledge you have that are particular to you:

* What are the things you know that no one else knows?
* What can you build that few others can?

It's likely that there are many ideas you could be good at executing, but you should focus on ideas where you have an unfair advantage compared to other founders; the idea where you have an edge.

There are two kinds of edge: problem edge or skills edge.

A problem edge comes from years experiencing a problem, working in an industry or having unique connections that enable you to fast track your problem knowledge. For example, Karin, a member of a previous EF cohort, had spent 10 years working in the translation industry and knew about the struggles to get high quality, fast translations. The startup she created solves these problems.

A skills edge often comes from years spent developing a rare or valuable skill. For example, Margara graduated from Sussex with a PhD in 3D character animation. She used the skills she had learnt to develop an augmented reality experience for kids.

At EF, individuals come to us with years of experience in certain industries (e.g., law, construction, retail) and then want to work on something they know very little about. Why does this happen? Often they know that the area they have expertise in is going to be tough to crack. However, this is an advantage. New industries seem easy, but it's only because you don't have enough expertise to know what the potential hurdles are.

So, ask yourself, of all your knowledge, what do you know most about? Of all your skills, which is the one that is most developed?

Then compare yourself to other potential founders in the space – can you compete?

If yes, then you've found your edge.

I wish you all the best for your journey!

Yours,
Alice

About the author:

Alice Bentinck is a British entrepreneur, technology consultant and blogger. She is the co-founder and COO of Entrepreneur First (EF), a London-based startup accelerator through which she supports Europe's best technical talent to build their own high-growth tech startups. The unique thing about EF is that individuals, who enter the programme don't need to have a team or an idea. Talent comes first. After finding only few women applying to EF, Alice set up Code First: Girls, a non-profit organisation, which provides free coding courses for women in university. In 2015, she was named one of the 'Fifty Most Inspiring Women in European Tech' by the Inspiring Fifty organisation and, in 2016, she was awarded an MBE for services to business by HRH Queen Elizabeth.

Letter No. 47

Heather Russell, Founder and CEO of Rinkya and Biscuit.io

Dear Female Founder,

Remember when you first started and you didn't have a huge network? It didn't matter back then because you built your business anyway. It doesn't really ever matter, I think.

Build a network and make friends because you like people, not because you are hoping to get something from them. Give to everyone you can, show people value and be helpful. It may or may not come back to you, but that doesn't matter, do it because that is what you are supposed to do.

It's really easy to make lots of mistakes when you are young, to blindly rush into things and to not think before acting. It's actually what got you here in the first place. However, reflect and learn from your past so you can make better decisions when you get older. When you get older, you will get tired, less tolerant, less willing to change as much; but those are things we have to fight against to be entrepreneurs. Always remember your past to improve your present.

When people give advice, they tend to project themselves on you – simply because they are drawing from their own experiences and that's the only thing they know. Be able to discern what is applicable to you and try to seek out people who are truly empathetic and can step into your shoes.

Advice doesn't take 10 minutes. It takes getting to truly know yourself and then truly getting to know another person.

Stay away from too much advice. Only YOU know your company, no one else does. The only steadfast advice I'll take is about my cap table. Cap tables are numbers and binary, but people are emotional. Investors are great, but just like you, sometimes *they* don't know what *they* are doing. Don't sign anything without getting someone you trust and who is knowledgeable to look at it. Make sure you learn what everything means in your contracts.

Challenge yourself, always. The minute you start getting complacent you risk stunting your growth. You need to constantly be growing, so please don't forget this or you'll wake up one day having realised you've been living in the Matrix and wasted a bunch of time.

You will be jealous and envious of others. It's normal and it's only human nature. Someone around the corner is jealous and envious of you. Don't compare yourself to others, or you will be miserable.

Focus on how you can make yourself better, and improve. You can't control anything but yourself. Being the best version of you means being introspective and constantly challenging yourself. We are constantly trying to improve our businesses, but what makes ourselves better? Yes, life is unfair, but how bad is your life, really? Sure, there are people all around who seem to just have things fall in their laps, but never mind others. Focus on you and focus on outcomes.

The only thing that matters are outcomes. Everything else is just vapor.

The last thing I will mention is something very important. You are not a girl or a boy, black or white, beautiful or ugly. You are first and foremost an entrepreneur. Don't stick yourself in the box you are supposed to be thinking outside of.

Love always,
Heather

About the author:

Heather Russell is a serial entrepreneur originally from Brooklyn, New York. At the age of 24, she moved to Japan, learned the language and built her second company Rinkya.com – a global eCommerce and logistics company. Heather lived in Japan for 12 years during which time she grew Rinkya into a multimillion-dollar business. She now resides in London and plays an active role as an advisor and mentor to the startup community, including Techstars and 500 Startups. Heather is now working on her third company, Biscuit.io, which is in the energy management sector.

Letter No. 48

MoJen Jenkins, Founder and Creative Director of The Noisemakers

Dear Female Founder,

My name is MoJen, and I'm the founder and creative director of The Noisemakers. It's been an exciting journey to get here, and I've had one hell of a ride so far.

I am the master of unrelated work experience. I've been a laboratory assistant, a salad chef, a swimming pool inspector, an IT consultant, a film composer, a sound designer, a roller derby coach and a web developer, and that's not even the whole list. I've also worked at McDonald's. I've worked for multinational corporations, mom-and-pop shops, and, most relevant to this letter, for myself. At the last count, I've founded seven companies and two of them are still running. In pursuit of all of this I've travelled to 19 countries and settled in two of them.

What I've learned along the way is that I'll never stop learning. Knowledge should be shared, and starfish can regenerate their limbs. With that in mind, here's my step-by-step, foolproof guide to founder success.

1. Take care of yourself

Meditate, journal, rest, and exercise. Sleep with purpose. Don't sit for long periods of time. Take regular breaks. Stand up straight and don't look down when you walk.

2. Eat well

Food is fuel, and we all need fuel. So eat like it counts. 'Eat well' means to make sure you enjoy it. Whatever you put in your face should make you happy. Mealtime is one guaranteed break that you get every day. Make sure this time is well spent.

3. Breathe deeply

Stop. Inhale. Exhale. Repeat.

4. Drink copious amounts water

The more water you drink, the more often you go to the toilet. This is the other guaranteed break that you get every day. Just saying.

5. Listen

Talking is easy. Listening is hard. How often are you thinking of your next point (or saying it) before the other person has finished speaking?

And… that's it. Were you expecting more?

Here is the thing. You're reading a letter to addressed to female founders, which means either you fall into this category already, or you are thinking about joining. So you have already taken the first step. Also, you are resourceful enough to do some research before you get started. That is the next important step, and you have already taken that too. So far, so good.

Now, how is this list going to get you from here to the next Y Combinator cohort, your unicorn valuation, your private helicopter and your Time Magazine cover? I understand that it may be difficult to see the relationship between your success and multiple trips to the toilet, so I'll explain.

The greatest barriers to the pursuit of a complex endeavour are simple. We may not want to do it, we may not have a compelling reason to do it, or we may think we are simply not able to do it. All of these barriers stem from what we don't know. We let what we don't know stop us instead of allowing what we do know to move us forward. Especially as women.

My list is made up of things you know. They are things you understand and that you may well be doing already. And they all help you be the best female founder you can be. That is my point: There is nothing about being a female founder that you can't do or aren't doing already. If there is something you don't know (or think you don't know), ask someone. Read a book. Google it. Everything under the sun has been done already, except for you. Bring your original ideas to the party, and let the rest of the guests help you make it a success. You already have everything you need to make it happen.

The last thing I'll leave you with is the concept of subjective success. For a 25-year-old, success is waking up on time for work after an epic night of partying. For a 95-year-old, success is waking up. It's all relative. Keep your definition malleable; let it grow and change as you do and stay successful. That's foolproof.

MJ

About the author:

MoJen Jenkins is an American entrepreneur in the creative industries who now resides in London. She is a lifelong noisemaker, part-time idealist, and creative-technical-business hybrid with 20+ years of eclectic experience in the entertainment industry. MoJen has worn many hats as a founder, vision holder, business developer, creative director, producer, coder and content creator. She was listed among Top 100 UK Women in Video Games by MCV Magazine in 2013 and was appointed a jury member of the 2015 and 2016 BAFTA Video Game Awards.

Letter No. 49

Narkis Alon, Co-Founder and Chief Creative Officer of Elevation Academy

Dear Female Founder,

First of all, I want to encourage you to always trust your intuition, while you embark on your entrepreneurial journey. The business world often gives more respect and legitimacy to the analytical logical side of ours, but as human beings we have two sides of the brain, so we better use both. Never forget: *Your intuition is there for a reason. Make sure to follow it.*

Secondly, I want to share with you how much I realised that everything in business is about people. Your team, partners, investors, customers – all of them are people who have their own states of mind, beliefs, agendas and feelings. The more you invest your energy in seeing things from their point of view, while keeping your goal in mind, the more you will be rewarded.

Thirdly, success is not an end goal. It is a never ending journey and built daily by accomplishing many small things. Ultimately, success is about the person you become while on that journey.

As I'm writing this, I am only 28 years old. I am still at the beginning of my own journey; yet, I have already achieved some things that I dreamt about since the age of five, which make me feel proud and 'successful'.

Start with one step and you will see. The more you do, the more you want to do. Remember to acknowledge your small wins, learn from the journey and always explore how you can grow – these are my ingredients for success.

Another thing that I have learnt as an entrepreneur is that we constantly think about what we still haven't done – our never-ending to-do lists. But sometimes the most magical and empowering moments happen when you realise that you already *are* where you want to be, and let yourself *be* in this seat that you created for yourself with a lot of hard work.

For me, these moments can happen when I meet with my team and we realise that we have achieved an ambitious goal against all odds or when we brought a crazy idea to life that touched thousands of hearts, or when I get emails from people sharing how our projects changed their lives and that they want my advice about the way they can integrate it to their own life.

For you, such a moment can happen when you suddenly meet a person who gets your idea. After hearing "No", "No" and another "No", you finally meet someone who thinks what you are doing is important and meaningful, and is willing to take a risk on you.

When you keep going after everyone told you to stop, you will understand the most wonderful thing entrepreneurship can teach you: It all depends on you.

True power comes from within. The outside world is only a reflection of the way you are inside; the way you think, the way you feel, your presence, and your intention. Make sure you invest time in developing your current state of mind to the state of mind of the person you wish to be, until one day – without noticing – you become that person.

And when you experience rough times, when your thoughts are negative and your mood is low, please don't be hard on yourself. Get up and start again. As Frank Sinatra sang: "Each time I find myself, flat on my face, I just lift my head up and get back in the race."

I love you for being in this journey and for living *your* journey. Make sure that you stay on your unique path, where your truth is. Other people's paths are already crowded enough.

Narkis

About the author:

Narkis Alon is an Israeli entrepreneur based in Tel Aviv. She is the co-founder and Chief Creative Officer of Elevation Academy, a technology and entrepreneurship academy that creates transformational learning experiences focused on online skills. She is a member of the steering committee for women empowerment of Tel-Aviv Municipality, founder of the Elevation W entrepreneurship programme. Prior to that, she co-founded Ze-Ze.org, an organization that empowers communities in need through creative and financially sustainable projects. Narkis was named 30 under 30 by Forbes Israel, Ford Fellow of the 92nd Street Y in 2014, a Schusterman fellow and is a member of the Global Shapers network of the World Economic Forum, where she co-founded Table for Two Israel. She blogs for the Huffington Post and speaks at international conferences such as Davos, TEDx, the Lift conference and more. She also served at Israel's 8200 elite intelligence unit of Israel Defense Forces (IDF) and holds a double major BA in Psychology and Film at Tel Aviv University.

Letter No. 50

Debbie Wosskow, Founder and CEO of Love Home Swap

Dear Female Founder,

I want to take some time to talk to you about time.

I know that – when you are young – it can seem like older people always seem to be going on about time and how precious it is. But that's not the kind of time I want to talk about.

I want to talk about the time we have every day and that how we choose to use that time shapes everything we are and everything we can be.

You can't stop time or slow it down, of course, but you can make it work for you. Good habits built in your youth can give you an edge for the rest of your life.

One of the most important things I could ever say to a young girl who wants to succeed in business is probably exactly the kind of advice that most young girls don't want to hear.

It is this: rise early every morning, and start working as soon as you can.

That one small thing (I know it can be tough) can turn a solid career into a great one. It can turn a good founder into a fantastically successful one.

I understand how a warm duvet on a cold and damp morning can seem the most attractive place in the world, but it really is a false reward. Because every minute, every hour you spend snuggling in that quilt is a minute and an hour you'll need to spend chasing back the rest of the day. And nobody works their best when chasing lost time.

But here is the key thing I want you to take note of. I'm not telling you that you should get up early so you can go on and work a killer 12 or 15-hour day. Quite the opposite. I'm saying that by getting up early and meeting the day on your terms you WON'T have to work that 15-hour killer day.

'Killer hours' are exactly that: killer. They take time away from your friends, time from your family and time away from doing the things you love. They sap you and wear you down. You become less like, not more like, the person you aspire to be. It even makes that duvet harder to get out of in the morning.

Slogging away 15 hours a day instead of eight doesn't make you a better worker either. I currently run a global business that allows me to travel the world and do what I love. But I make sure to leave the office every day at 5:30pm sharp.

In my career as a founder, I have built two successful businesses this way. And for all the education I have, all the skills I have built, all the technology I use, rising early is as important as any of it.

Working with time, not against it, makes you a more efficient person, which makes you a more successful person, which makes you a happier person. Every minute you are in control of is worth countless times more than a minute that is controlling you.

What's more, if you feel like you were the best you could be at the end of every day, then that gives you even more inspiration to bounce out of bed the next morning and do it all over again.

The more you learn to beat that morning temptation to stay under the covers, the more you can enjoy life later. Because you will be working on your terms, not the clock's.

So to the young female founder reading this, no technology will ever be as helpful to your career as an alarm clock.

It can be tough being an early riser, but trust me, the rewards will come. It's just a matter of time.

With love,
Debbie

About the author:

Debbie Wosskow is a British serial entrepreneur and global authority on digital disruption and its impact on markets, businesses, and working practices. Debbie has particular expertise in the digital trend 'access over ownership'. She started her first business at the age of 25 and successfully scaled the marketing company before selling it to the network, the Loewy Group. Now on her second business, Debbie founded and runs Love Home Swap, the world's largest home swapping club. A renowned supporter of the global digital industry, Debbie is also the founding chair of the trade body, Sharing Economy UK and regularly advises and invests in startups (often female run) helping them to make their idea become a reality. Debbie was named one of the original '35 under 35' women to watch in 'Management Today' and was also awarded an OBE for services to business by HRH Queen Elizabeth.

Letter No. 51

Nancy Fechnay, Co-Founder of The Inspire Movement

Dear Female Founder,

My name is Nancy LaMaster Fechnay. I am a founder, an advisor, and an investor.

My professional journey began with earning an engineering degree from the University of Virginia in the United States. At 23, I started my first company and at 30, my second. In between, I worked as an investor and consultant. I went on to earn a Masters of Business Administration from Duke University's Fuqua School of Business. Since moving to the UK, my career has been full of investing in startups, advising various companies, and launching a startup of my own.

Through my education and work background I have learned some valuable lessons about life and business. Let's jump in…

Find incredible mentors.

In my life, I have been blessed with genuine, successful, courageous, and wise advisors. I attribute a great deal of my life's successes to those individuals. I have learned to never underestimate the power of surrounding yourself with smart people who *care* about you and your future.

Your advisors must understand your challenges and have a vested interest in you as a person. If you are a founder, find an advisor or mentor that has started a company before. If you want to become a venture capitalist, befriend an investor to teach and help you.

Dare to think big.

Many founders are only concerned with the problems they see locally. When running Duke Ventures, I saw countless founders thinking solely about the east coast market. In the UK, founders often focus solely on the UK market.

However, one should take the time to think from the first day what will happen when the venture expands to the next market. The successful founder must think about questions such as "How will my model need to change?" and "How can I prepare for that now?"

While starting my first business, I did not know that I should be concerned with those types of questions aforementioned; I too had a narrow vision. I only dealt with what was immediately in front of me. I never considered or planned for the long term. I urge everyone to be wiser and plan ahead.

If you struggle with this, then find someone who is strong at it. It really is important to surround yourself with those who make you better. If your business is not sustainable at the end of the day, then all of your effort and hard labor put forth in the present will be wasted in the future.

Share. Give back.

One of the most incredible things about Silicon Valley and San Francisco is the culture of sharing, and I do not mean the 'sharing economy'. I am referring to free flowing information, advice, opinions, hacks, contacts, and everything else similar!

As you build your company, those around you will be the ones who become your founder family – embrace them, help them, share with them. In 5 years time, you will look back on how much you have learned from your founder family. You will be grateful that you contributed because of what you received in return, exponential growth and learning.

There is nothing wrong with needing help. In some cultures, admitting that you cannot do it by yourself is unacceptable. Entrepreneurship is not one of those cultures. In entrepreneurship, that admission is a must.

Be honest.

Honesty is an important characteristic no matter the industry, but in entrepreneurship, honesty is vital. The startup world may seem huge, but it is a very small community. It is like being back in high school – word travels fast and people are unforgiving.

For example, when raising capital do not tell one firm you are talking to another firm, when you are not. It sounds so simple, yet that lie is told all the time. Investors are entrusting you, the founder, with their fund's money. Do not give them a reason to mistrust you.

Build up your mental and emotional strength.

Running a startup comes with lots of emotional challenges. Be ready for many highs and lows. Develop thick skin, because you will get knocked down many times. But successful people are those who always get back up and keep pushing.

There will be days where you will feel 'low', but you will need to go through those days with no loss of enthusiasm. To be successful, you must remain positive in the face of adversity and sometimes, you have to be almost borderline arrogant. You are going to be told "No" so many times, that it is going to be extremely difficult to pull through, if you are not mentally and emotionally strong.

Lastly, you will experience situations when everybody has a different opinion on what you should be doing next. You will be confused listening to contradicting advice, but you have to remember to rely on your gut.

Starting up your own business is both nerve wrecking and rewarding. It will shape you tremendously as a person. I wish you all the best on this exciting journey!

Yours truly,
Nancy

About the author:

Nancy Fechnay is an American founder, investor, mentor, and advisor for startups and accelerators, based in London, UK. She is the co-founder of The Inspire Movement, a new community of entrepreneurs and thought leaders, who have been through adversity and emerged transformed for the better. She is also a Partner at Flight Ventures, the largest online group of investors in the world, where she oversees UK operations. Additionally, she is an advisor to several U.S. and UK early-stage startups. Nancy has worked for several US-based investment firms, including Kleiner Perkins Caufield & Byers, GE Ventures, and Core Capital Partners. She is the co-founder Duke Ventures, a venture capital educational and deal-sourcing engine that advises founders on business strategy and highlights the best Duke startups to a network of active investors. Nancy has a Bachelor of Science degree in Systems Engineering (University of Virginia), an MBA focused on entrepreneurship (Duke), and a Masters in Environmental Management focused on energy (Duke).

Letter No. 52

Nur Al Fayez, Co-Founder and CEO of Feesheh.com

Dear Female Founder,

A couple of months ago, I was interviewed about what it is like to be a female entrepreneur and I answered the following:

"I never thought of myself as a 'female' founder. It could be easier for male entrepreneurs in many ways, but entrepreneurship is full of obstacles, so it's never easy for either males or females. It's there for the crazy ones who choose not to see the obstacles and have faith in a greater vision. As an entrepreneur, you go beyond your own limits, becoming a moving force rather than a regular human with personal needs. You transform spiritually into a force that evolves and adapts constantly for the mission you believe in accomplishing."

The force that you become has no gender and no eyes to see all the challenges you will encounter. As you focus on the light at the end of the tunnel, you will stay blind to the stereotypes in other people's heads. No one can stop you, but your own self.

No one will ever tell you "*as a woman* you can't do this", they would just say "you can't do it". And exactly here, you will start doubting yourself on a deep level.

The one golden rule I could give you is: do not doubt yourself and sharpen your consciousness when somebody criticises you. Do no let criticism crush you. Learn to understand when it is constructive and when it is purely driven by bias. Either way, take it and learn from it. Grow into a stronger person with a greater purpose each and every day.

Are you worrying about how you look and how you talk, and wanting to be perceived as 'serious'? Don't try to be someone you are not.

Are you multitasking to prove that you can do it all? Surround yourself by a team you really trust, ask for help whenever you need, and utilise your close and extended network.

Are you looking for a role model to stay inspired, and you are looking extra hard for female ones? Role models are not always under the spotlight. Stay close to other entrepreneurs; they are what you need to be inspired.

Are you going through a lot of imbalances and burnouts? Lead a healthy lifestyle: eat right, sleep well, and exercise. Make time for it. There is time.

Whenever your doubts creep up again, look into the mirror and say, "I can do it".

All the best to your future,
Nur

About the author:

Nur Al Fayez is a Jordanian entrepreneur based in Amman. She is the co-founder and CEO of Feesheh.com, the first online one-stop-shop for musicians in the Middle East & North Africa region. Nur won the 1st place in Jordan at Seedstars World competition for emerging markets and was accepted into the 500 Startups accelerator programme in San Francisco. She is an architect by degree and a marketer by passion. She is also a vocalist and performed previously with the Jordanian National Choir. In 2015, Alfayez launched her second venture Startup Band, a musical launchpad that gathers musical talents and challenges them to create a band, persona, and song in 48 hours.

Letter No. 53

Reshma Sohoni, Co-Founder and Partner of Seedcamp

Dear Female Founder,

I am writing to you as a founding partner of Seedcamp, where I invest in early-stage tech startups from around the world. I am grateful to be surrounded by intelligent, ambitious people from many different backgrounds building the big companies of tomorrow. But I have come a long way.

It has been a long way since I left high school and started my degrees in Business and Engineering at the University of Pennsylvania in the US – and a very long way from the sleepy city of Pune, India, where I was born. I have continued to be fiercely determined throughout my career and with luck and preparation I have seized on some wonderful opportunities to get me where I am.

Looking back on my journey, the biggest piece of advice I can offer you is to totally immerse yourself in new people, new ideas and new concepts. The unknown is the most exhilarating thing out there. Make an effort to grow the mountain of discovery, and you will be immensely happy and become a good person at the same time.

This is something I now do daily, and I wish I had a chance to do so sooner. Look for multidisciplinary people to learn from. The world in which you are working now provides you with a community of makers and dreamers. Enjoy being part of it.

Look to understand the unknown, as early as you can. Question things you don't understand. Find interesting communities that will allow you to broaden your knowledge of the world. The world is positive and filled with great things, but reality is very different from the life of school. Get out there. Learn what the real world implications of your choices will be. Relish the unknown and broaden your views.

Another big piece of advice is to take time to save money. I was lucky enough to travel the world many times over and experience fantastic things that gave me pleasure and happiness. But I have realised that saving more will make a bigger impact further down the road than it does in the enjoyment of daily pleasures. Be mindful of that along your journey. The world can change dramatically, so save and invest early – and you will reap the rewards for time to come!

Your health is your biggest asset in life. Keep up running, racing, and eating healthily. Also love your family and friends deeply and spend a lot of time with them. It's the one thing you will never regret in life. No matter how successful you are, the most important things are your health and your family and friends. Never lose sight on them.

Oh and just a couple of other bits. Remember to enjoy the small pleasures in life we can so often take for granted! For me, I wish I'd learnt to cook – it would have been a great favor for my family. I also wish I'd had more time to discover music, and really appreciate great TV and films. Creativity is a wonderful part of being human and we should make time to appreciate it, using it to escape and open up new ideas within ourselves.

While you are busy being a founder, don't forget to live a life too.

All my best,
Reshma

About the author:

Reshma Sohoni is an Indian-American investor based in London. She is the co-founder and partner of Seedcamp, a First Round Fund, backing pre-seed and seed stage tech startups from around the world. She brings a good mix of tech, commercial drive, and American chutzpah to the team. Reshma has always combined technology and business from university to today. She started her career in M&A and venture capital across B2B Software and Internet services businesses in the US and India, then went to INSEAD and earned her MBA. She fell in love with Europe and stayed on to work in Commercial and Marketing Strategy at Vodafone. Starting Seedcamp in 2007 was a once in a lifetime opportunity, which she jumped into. Her main role at Seedcamp today is helping companies with fundraising and business development.

Letter No. 54

Tia Kansara, Founder and Director of Kansara Hackney Ltd

Dear Female Founder,

In youth we have chances we often miss. The reason why some people get ahead in our eyes is because they were aware of themselves and what they wanted more than we did. But today, there are amazing opportunities to design the life *you* want to live.

The only thing that can ever limit you is you. Never let someone else's limitations become yours. The road ahead is a clear one, if you believe so. The road ahead is filled with obstacles, if you believe so.

What changes your perspective is your observation. How can you take an opportunity to the next level, if you don't even see it? Invest in your ability to observe better and nurture your ability to understand and interpret a moment better. This opens doors in the immediate. There is no remorse like the opportunity you wish you had seen quicker.

Also, time is relative. You can be the master of your time. If I gave you 8 hours, every minute and every second – what would you do with it? That's what success is. Spending every second the way you want to. Productivity and success in these moments is judged only by yourself. If you want to spend 10 hours singing, and you then go ahead to spend the full 10 hours singing, then this is success. So the question is, how do you want to spend every second? The answer only lies within you. Yes, there are clues, signs and nudges that your exterior world can give you, but all this is useless until your inner wisdom is awakened.

If there's something I have learnt that has helped me tremendously, it is the ability to be still. Recognise every sensation and feeling that you have, and every gesture that is peculiar around you. Some people say "everything happens for a reason", but the 'reason' is whatever you assign to something. Upon self-reflection you would perhaps see things differently; so give yourself time to reflect.

We live in multiple dimensions. Each dimension (seen and unseen) exposed to our actions bears a Karmic response that is attached to our being. Be very careful about what you put out in the world. My mentor would often tell me: "Be polite to whoever you are passing on the ladder going up, chances are – they will be going up when you are coming down, and they will remember you".

Your strength lies in the cultivation of your dreams. A dream is a wish unless you have a plan to turn it into reality. Imagine and be creative with what you want, these thoughts become ingredients of the meal that you will eat. The sensation you will get from thinking of something profound and then actualising it is what life is worth living for.

Whatever you want to do, start early. While you go after what you want from life, make sure to put conscious efforts into maintaining your mental, physical and spiritual fitness daily. Make it a point to imbibe your favourite activities and grow these areas of your life. The scariest thing is waking up and realising you can't even touch your toes!

Last but not least, use your natural drug store! It's all there, in your body. There are regions inside you that can give everlasting peace and joy.

These are accessible through meditation and energy healing. Take some time to learn more about the experiences your body can give to you.

Regrets are for other people. You feel like doing it, do it. There is no time like the present!

Yours,
Tia

About the author:

Tia Kansara is a British entrepreneur and sustainability specialist. She is the founder and director of Kansara Hackney Ltd, a leading consulting firm that is specialised in sustainable lifestyle and design. As its youngest consultant, Tia was invited to advise the United Nations Conference on Trade and Development, BioTrade Initiative on sustainability. She holds a Ph.D. degree at University College London on the design of future cities and is fluent in many languages (Gujarati, Japanese, Hindi, Urdu, Sanskrit, French, Arabic and English). She is also Chair of the Thousand Network, a community of 1000 leading change-makers as well as the UCL Bartlett Ambassador for the Gulf region. Tia is also an advanced deep-sea diver, a Physical Training Instructor (British Territorial Army) and classical Hindi vocalist. In her spare time, she enjoys travelling and reading.

Letter No. 55

Tine Thygesen, Serial Entrepreneur and Professional Board Member

Dear Female Founder,

Recently, I was in a room filled with talented women in London. It was a private equity conference for women and I had been skeptical about accepting the offer to speak. I'm not generally a fan of female business networks, as I just want to grow my business, not make a political statement, and as such I prefer to mix with people of influence, also when they happen to be men.

Much to my surprise, the event was inspirational. These women weren't meek. They were successful, and they were sharing their war stories about being a woman in business openly and candidly. My favorite was a managing partner being asked to negotiate a huge business deal from behind a curtain in the Middle East because of the fact that she was a woman. The room was roaring with laughter and the energy was tangible. These women were powerful and successful and they were having no more of being considered second best. It was invigorating.

This is how we have to change the status quo – by being strong. We need to stop the narrative of women being weaker creatures who need special terms to compete. We can be powerful and successful without being masculine. But we need to change the rules in business to enable female leadership, so that we can create strong role models.

On my panel was Julie Meyer, CEO of Ariadne Capital, and she summed it up perfectly when she said, "Don't break someone else's glass ceiling, own your own ceiling".

This is the essential truth about women in general. We play too much by the rules. Rather than staying in a position where the current power structure makes it unlikely for you to rise to the top, make your own power structure. Change the rules. Don't follow the expected path.

For my own part, I have now been the CEO of four companies and I sit on several board of directors. I got to there by taking an untraditional approach. Otherwise, I would have never made it.

I arrived in London 15 years ago with nothing but a basic diploma and the desire to take on the world. I ended up with a job in investment banking despite no finance qualifications. An American bank needed the five languages I spoke more than standard finance qualifications and gave me the job, which became my first step on the career ladder. I was terrified on my first day, but I took the chance.

Later, at another bank, the head of HR came by my desk asking me to bring my university degree for her to have on file. "I don't have any. I haven't really found time for university yet", I replied, surprised and slightly embarrassed. She looked like her world had just tumbled. "But we don't hire people without a degree!" she cried out. But it was a bit too late to fire me, especially as it was her own mistake – not asking to see my degree in the first place – and I was doing my job well. So she let it be and taught me my second lesson: apply for great jobs, even if you don't tick all the boxes.

When I moved to New Zealand, I wasn't even able to get an interview with the local banks, because they considered my specialised London banking experience irrelevant for the smaller market. My father-in-law insisted that I call the CEOs directly. I was so embarrassed, but I had no alternative plan. So I wrote a personal letter to each of the CEOs. Sure enough, one of the CEOs invited me to his office for coffee and a chat about how I could help his bank expand. That would have never happened, if I had gone the traditional way.

When I started my first company in Australia, I was in my mid-twenties and people used to be so impressed with the young age and the CEO title. It sounds like a gimmick, but once you have the title – or a position of power – you are perceived differently and given the chance to prove what you're made of. It's still insanely hard work, but you have just given yourself the chance to shine.

The point here is that you have to take charge of yourself. When the rules are not in your favour, don't play by them.

Whether we like it or not, there is a world of unconscious bias against women. So every time you stray away from being nice, warm or pretty, you will elicit a negative response. That is what happens at the playground when domineering boys are attributed with 'leadership potential' but domineering girls are 'bossy'. It is the effect of thousands of years of inequality between genders, and it's not going to change overnight. An ambitious woman needs to move beyond that, and teach herself not to take notice or be hurt.

So if we are to change the world that our daughters will inherit, we need to change the perception of women being second-class leaders – quietly, consistently, by over-performing, doing a kick-ass job and promoting other women.

It is possible, but it requires that women disregard the existing power setup, when it works against them, and that we all start building new power structures when needed.

So take charge of your own journey and let's make it happen! Rather than waiting passively, be proactive and start getting your life on the track you want it to be on.

Yours,
Tine

About the author:

Tine Thygesen is an entrepreneur based in Copenhagen. She is a professional board member and serial entrepreneur with a proven track record. She is a well-known thought leader in mobile, modern leadership and entrepreneurship, and speaks at events all over the world. She is internationally recognized for her work – named among Top 10 Tech Speakers in Europe, Top 100 Women in Tech in Europe and Talent100 in Denmark. For 10 years, Tine has been creating scalable new technology products and companies, working with all stages of venture development. Highly internationally minded, she has lived in 6 countries and acquired customers in 200 countries. Tine's passions are champagne, maps, design, new companies, tribes, castles, behavioral economics and building brands. In no particular order.

Letter No. 56

Alyssa Jade McDonald-Bärtl, Founder and CEO of BLYSS, CACAOacademy and ChangeMakerLand

Dear Female Founder,

Rather than discussing the ongoing fight for existence as founders which we as women often find ourselves in, within this letter to you I suggest we should be allowing ourselves the grace to make mistakes as we grow into our own entrepreneurial shoes. That, dear founder friend, will help attract the resources you require to facilitate growth.

I often remind myself to actually forget what my would-be, should-be and could-be expertise is, and form unique decisions according to my mindset instead. With mindset, I mean my habitual thoughts and feelings that form a lens through which I see the world, my industry and my company.

I would like to share two of my most powerful mindsets with you. Both have helped me grow beyond the start-up phase of my first business and enabled me to create additional businesses also.

Loss As An Asset

Whenever we make mistakes and lose something unbeknownst to ourselves we are actually creating the greatest assets in our business. Whether it's deciding on a partnership, choosing a manufacturing process, targeting a certain niche; whatever the decision might be, if things end up in a red loss, they can and often do turn into our best assets.

Decisions leading to failure are the best learning curve, helping us get closer to the mark next time. In this regard, my company is very asset rich as I have made a lot of mistakes over the years. In fact, we literally have boxes of 'assets' sitting in a storage building as static reminders of things I have misjudged.

In the beginning, I used to try to leverage these and re-use, 're-wire' so to speak. However, I found out that just letting go of the loss was usually the best way to go. I learnt not to attempt to try to salvage a loss at the cost of a new idea or a fresh direction.

My mindset towards loss is clear now. I make a mistake, I stop the haemorrhage, cordon off the loss, sell what is still salvageable, and sink the rest. Everything turns into an asset in learning. I learn from it, but I don't look back.

And in case you are wondering about the boxes of 'assets' mentioned earlier: I still have 30,000 custom made beautiful tin packagings left over from the first Blyss product launched years ago. That mistake made my business what it is today, as have the hundreds of other over and underestimations I made about supplies, demands, customers and production. No one is perfect, least of all an entrepreneur, but what I have learned is that good entrepreneurs learn from their mistakes, take the knocks and move on.

Humble Expertise

When we start a business, people are quick to call us experts. I have often found it difficult to strike the balance between 'humbly learning about my business and industry' and 'being a full expert'.

The corporate world teaches us to put titles like 'XYZ Manager', or 'Subject Matter Expert' on our name tags. In the startup world, however, we have a whole new set of operating methods and levels we never knew existed. Even when we are seasoned industry veterans, we do not need to wear the 'armour' of competence. In fact, when we do this, what we are really doing is creating a pressure cooker to hurt ourselves with later.

I refuse to be deemed an 'expert' because people expect experts to have everything fully worked out. But I realised quickly (and painfully) that you will always have gaps in knowledge in the complex world we live in and that it's impossible to have all the answers worked out.

So be careful with what you put on a Twitter bio, on Linkedin pages etc., and allow yourself space to experience a graceful learning curve as you develop. Following 8 years of having my own social enterprises, my bio reads that I 'share standards and tools to evolve sovereignty and agroecology in cacao'. I do not label myself a 'chocolate expert', 'social enterprise expert' or anything of that nature. Instead, I position myself as a passionate champion, humbly do my best, and know that my action contributes to something meaningful.

Underselling the expert role has a lot to do with focusing on my intent and mission. I found this, as a method to generate new business models, a softer way to enter markets, and also to give myself some leeway when it comes to making inevitable mistakes.

As you probably know by now, you don't have to be the best at what you do in order to have a great business. However, what you must be is resilient, continually standing up for what you believe in, and learning from the mistakes that might set you back.

This business of yours, or mine, will not continue to succeed generation after generation, because it is rocket science amazing. It will succeed because we have put a humble growth strategy in place that allows us to recover from mistakes and puts our learning and contributions forward.

Through continuous learning, we will attract the resources and people we need to get closer to being stellar and insightful. With a good dose of humility in our position as a startup, we soon will find ourselves running with the giants, advising industry panels and even shaping legislation. I never thought that this is what I would be doing with a little idea to farm great cacao and support wonderful chocolatiers, however, my business evolved from those two simple mindsets.

Stay agile, stay humble. See loss as asset and present yourself as a passionate advocate, and you will attract the help you need to see the goals through. Forget the job titles and the plates of armour, they will be heavy to stand in when you have fallen a few times. It is normal to fall, but abnormal for us to burden ourselves and be heavy.

Love,
Lyss

About the author:

Alyssa Jade McDonald-Bärtl is a third generation social entrepreneur working to evolve standards influencing food sovereignty and agroecology. Currently she farms and delivers cacao from both South America and South Asia, running 3 humble enterprises, BLYSS, CACAOacademy and ChangeaMakerLand from Europe to the Middle East. She is the wife of a Bavarian, daughter of Papua New Guinean and a devout friend. She speaks Australian styles of English and German, which together come across as something more like Denglish. She is also a board member of Unternehmensgrün, the German Federal Association of Green Economy, as well as a founding board member of Ecopreneur. eu, the European Sustainable Business Federation, where she stands for topics of start up, social enterprise and International business.

Letter No. 57

Julia Jacobson, Co-Founder and CEO of NMRKT

Dear Female Founder,

Nothing can prepare you for the experience of founding a startup.

A friend of mine, who recently launched a company, said the biggest surprise was what she learned about herself. When you work at a large organization, there are standards and systems in place that can gear you up for success. You execute your job well and then get promoted – the cycle continues to pat you on the back and build your confidence. When you start your own business, however, you are suddenly smacked in the face with all the things that you are not great at. The faster you can adjust and accept this, the better you will feel about startup life.

The truth is: You cannot fully anticipate or prepare for the overwhelming weight that you will bear as a startup founder. Reading this now will certainly help, but there are some things in life that you will have to experience first-hand to fully understand.

Being a startup founder means sacrificing it all for the vision. Running a marathon on empty; financially strapped, physically exhausted, with no time for fun or friends, on a roller coaster of rejection and deep responsibility. One moment a big win, the next a catastrophic loss.

Every month, I go for a 'walk and talk' with a founder friend. He always asks, "How are things?" and I always say "The usual, amazing and awful all at once". He agrees. It's not a female founder thing; it's the roller coaster that everyone is on. No one is an exception.

But female founders have one more weight to bear. Our gender.

"One of these things is not like the other" is the hard reality you live as a female founder. You are not like 'them' and everyone makes sure you know it.

In our physical appearance, our demeanor, the tone and pitch of our voice, our personality, our behaviour, and our way of thinking – we are different. We are women.

For years, men have dominated the technology world. And not just men, but a very specific personality type. Pattern recognition has been engrained into the minds, lives and ways of operating in the industry. From fellow founders to VCs, it perpetuates itself.

I was recently at a female founder dinner with a well-known female VC. On the subject of facing the challenge of pattern recognition she bragged about coaching her female CEOs to pitch like a man.

My heart sunk.

As a startup founder, and particularly as a female founder, people will judge you and try to define you. I have been called too girly, too old, too youthful, too energetic, too passionate. None fit the pattern.

There's so much I didn't know when starting my company. I could give you advice on how to 'play the game', tell you that integrity is everything or even how to pitch like a man. But none of that is important.

In the end, all that matters is you. No company is worth sacrificing who you are.

The weight a startup founder carries is enough to break a person. But add the 'outside' feeling of being a woman and you have a recipe for confidence shattering. I let it get the best of me too many times.

I was a high heel wearing girly girl. I played ball with the boys – from Advanced Placement math classes to the top of the promotional ladder. I was confident, extroverted and got things done.

Until I let the name calling, the weight of responsibility and the feeling of being an outsider get to me.

I unconsciously began to change my appearance, my friends and my interests to fit in. Not all bad changes. But one day I looked in the mirror and didn't recognize myself. I had focused so much on the 'founder' version of me that I lost the other parts that made me who I was.

I called a mentor. I was crying and rattling off the reasons why I shouldn't be running the company. Why the problem was me, not the business.

I forgot what she told me exactly, but the bottom line is: It's not you. It's the fit. And there's a big difference between the two.

At the beginning of the Techstars programs, David Cohen tells the founders that raising money is like dating. It's not 'you' and it's not 'him/her', it's how the two of you fit together.

Don't ever forget that. Even in moments of desperation.

Could your business model need improvement? Sure. Is your market opportunity too small? Possibly. But when the name calling starts and the negativity is turned on you, remember they are trying to say "We don't fit". It took Mark Zuckerberg over a hundred investors before he found his fit.

I'm not too girly to run this business. I'm not too old or too youthful to be a CEO. I'm not too passionate or energetic to succeed. I'm the smart, confident, capable woman who had the courage to start this company and who will see it through to the end.

Don't let their words define you. Don't let yourself be coached into pitching like a man. Don't retire your wardrobe to don the startup uniform. Don't stop smiling and stop taking time to have fun.

Be you. Embrace your quirks, your uniqueness, and your femininity. Whoever you are, own it. It's what got you here in the first place and it's the only thing that will get you over the finish line.

All my best,
Julia

About the author:

Julia Jacobson an American entrepreneur based in New York. She is the co-founder and CEO of NMRKT (pronounced: 'in market'), a Techstars alumni company, which makes it simple for any content creator to launch their own shop and monetise their influence. Julia graduated from Brown University with honors in 2007 and joined the executive program at Bloomingdale's. As a buyer, she handled three men's accessory departments nationwide with a profit & loss responsibility over

$6 million. Julia is a retail and e-commerce expert who has consulted for top tier trade shows and brands. She is also a mentor to Startup Weekend, Endeavor and Columbia University and Brown University entrepreneurial programs.

Letter No. 58

Sarah Nadav, Founder and CEO of Civilize

Dear Female Founder,

I'm Sarah Nadav, founder of two financial sector startups and mother to two boys. I was raised to believe that I could do anything and be anything, but I didn't have a lot of career ambition. I thought I had the choice between a career and children, but then life turned out otherwise – staying home with my kids became a luxury that I couldn't afford.

With two young children, who needed me, I went out into the world ready to use the talents, skills and education that my parents had the foresight to make sure I developed as a young adult. I thought that this would be enough.

I am a passionate problem solver (and a little bit of a weirdo), so being an entrepreneur came naturally to me. Now it is hard to imagine that there was ever a time, when I didn't know that I would love this.

Here is some advice for your journey: being an entrepreneur demands more than talent and ability. It demands the courage to deal with excessive amounts of stress and ambiguity. You have to constantly put your time and energy into projects, and most of the time they are going to fail.

'Failing' has become a catchphrase of the industry, which moves fast and breaks things. Learn how to fail and keep your soul intact. If you are a natural born overachiever, then work on that, because the consequences can be devastating.

As a woman, I feel like I have a duty to warn you that this is going to be a lot harder than you expect. The tech industry is not a meritocracy. You will need to dig deep and be brave to face the onslaught of sexism that currently permeates the industry.

The most important thing is actually knowing that this is real and happening. It is not in your head, or just being complained about by a bunch of cranky women who couldn't hack it. You will go to events that are attended mostly by men, sit in the audience and listen to men talk, sit across the table from male investors, and you need to know that they are judging you as inferior. They will hit on you, diminish your ideas and if you let that in, it will destroy you self-esteem.

So build a wall. A big one, a high one, and keep all of the haters on the other side. See through the situation as it is, and accept that it is real and true, but that it cannot stand. The future does not belong to young, white men. It belongs to a diverse group of people, who are courageous enough to fight to make a place for their voices to be heard and their projects to be built.

Reach out to people with diverse backgrounds and build networks with them, because they will be your allies, and you can be theirs. We need the solidarity, because we are all in this together.

Most of all, don't sideline your life goals for your career goals. I started on this journey with two kids, and raising them has been part of what keeps me sane and motivated. You will need a corner of your life where you are not judged by your success or failure, but rather loved unconditionally. That will sustain you.

Stay focused and aim true.

Best of luck,
Sarah

About the author:

Sarah Nadav is a startup CEO, social entrepreneur, Google mentor and journalist based in Tel Aviv, Israel. Her career has spanned a number of different iterations, but what they all have in common is the use of her creative skills to solve problems and engage people in a shared mission. Her latest venture is Civilize, a consumer advocacy and communications platform for people in debt, which got accepted into the Barclays Techstars Fintech Accelerator in Tel Aviv. Sarah was given an award from the Israeli Ministry of the Environment for 'Outstanding Volunteer Achievement' in recognition of her efforts founding and running a grassroots organisation called Atid Yarok (Green Future). She holds a Master's degree in Non-Profit/Public/Organizational Management from The Hebrew University.

Letter No. 59

Priscilla Elora Sharuk, Co-Founder and COO at myki

Dear Female Founder,

My name is Priscilla and I am the co-founder of myki.co.

A couple of years ago, while working for a luxury landscape architecture firm in Beirut, my friend turned co-founder Antoine and I had an idea. What started off as a simple "Imagine if we could log into our accounts without a password" turned slowly but surely into myki – the future of identity management.

Starting a company is a whirlwind, an adventure, perhaps even a voyage, and the highlight of it all: a continuous learning process. I had reached a plateau in my learning curve as an architect. The job was still challenging, but I just wasn't in the right place anymore. I needed to take myki from conception to execution, just like I had done in architecture. I felt equipped and so I quit my job and took the leap.

My father always urged me to be a 'flying trapeze' instead of a 'falling trapeze'. What he meant by that was that I should not let go of the first bar before I caught the other. But I took the leap anyway. There was no way of knowing what was in store for me, but I also couldn't live with myself, if I didn't try.

Here are a few things that I have learned along the way, which I would like to share with you to carry on your voyage:

Pitch, please! Your pitch is your investment ticket. The right content portrays your understanding of what drives your business, appealing visuals reveal an attention to detail, an integral facet of a successful entrepreneur, and a captivating delivery exposes your confidence in your product and vision. Pitch, iterate, and repeat, please!

You will never have all the answers. Entrepreneurship is not for everyone and if it was easy, everybody would do it. Waiting until everything is clear in your mind to go out there and share? Don't. It will never be clear. If you think you know it all, you are doing something wrong. Take risks.

There is no such thing as destructive criticism. Afraid to share your idea and get feedback? Then stay at home. Want to build a company? Then get out there, get out of your comfort zone and get as much feedback you can. Understand how different minds perceive your product, and learn to accept criticism in all its forms. The sooner you do, the better off you will be. Whatever people say, never take it personally.

Prepare for success. When you pitch, omit that one piece of information that you know is integral to your business, so when potential investors ask you about it, you have got the answer immediately! Congratulations, you have made it one step closer to that investment ticket. That one question may be your unique chance to wow the panel. Better anticipate it and impress, than freeze and stutter.

Value time. In this day and age, it is not who can do it better; it is who can do it faster. Time management is a key skill to master. Setting a time frame and adhering to it is proof you can deliver to yourself, your investors, and your potential customers. Also, you cannot improve what you cannot measure. Focus on getting things done day by day and you will be surprised at how much you can achieve within a month.

I believe that sharing what you continue to learn on your journey as an entrepreneur is integral to the growth and progress of an entire ecosystem. I urge you to share your successes, but more importantly, share your failures. That is how you and those around you grow, together.

Yours truly,
Priscilla

About the author:

Priscilla Elora Sharuk is a Lebanese entrepreneur based in Beirut. She is the co-founder and COO at myki, an enterprise mobile application that eliminates the need for usernames and passwords. She is also the creator of pitchplease.me, an initiative that helps entrepreneurs optimise their pitch deck in its visuals, content and delivery. She won Seedstars Beirut in 2014 and has been named one of the Top 20 Entrepreneurs in Science and Technology by Executive Magazine. Priscilla studied Landscape Design and Eco-Management at the American University of Beirut and was a sub-consultant of world renowned Architect Zaha Hadid before becoming a leading name in the fast-growing Lebanese tech startup scene.

Letter No. 60

Renata George, Venture Capitalist and Co-Founder of Women.VC community

Dear Female Founder,

What do you feel when you hear that women are tremendously underrepresented in whatever field you can think of? Whether it is in movies, executive business positions, funded ventures, science or as university deans; the statistics can be quite depressing and you might wonder: *"What are we all still doing wrong?"*

This is a fair question, but unfortunately, boiling over it has not proven to be effective to change the status quo in the last decade. Instead of focusing on the problem, I would like you to focus on a solution.

One solution could be: forget about the inequality that we inherited from times when women didn't even had the right to vote – and zoom into today's success stories!

This is what we did at Women.VC, an initiative of showcasing women venture capitalists from around the world, as well as breading the new generation of venture capitalists.

We decided to show how many women in venture capital we really have, how many startups they have backed, and how high the returns on their investments are. And guess what? It is not as bad as you would think. There are hundreds of women taking investment decisions in the

US alone. They have backed thousands of startups and their returns on investments are positive.

We are making small steps towards equal representation in our remit, and if you look closely enough, I'm sure you will find many driven women also in your field. Learn from them as much as you can.

Additionally, I would also like to give you a completely different view on the issue of female leadership – *a cultural view.*

Did you know that, according to Grant Thornton's International Business Report, a whopping 40% of executive business positions in Central and Eastern Europe are held by women? This is the highest percentage of women in senior management in the world!

Why is that the case? Let's dive into history to understand more.

Slavic women lived through centuries of monarchy, where men were the sole rulers with absolute and unlimited power. That was not only the political structure of society, but also a frame for commercial and family relationships. Slavic women always worked and supported their men, and the imperial mindset still exists today amongst Slavic female millennials. It is the norm for a man to lead with his woman behind him. This is all we have known, historically and culturally.

When the monarchy was overthrown, the Slavic woman stepped into the era of wars. She would lose her grandfather, father and elder brother to the war, leaving her with no choice but to change her lifestyle. These formative years bred strong self-sufficient women, as there were very few men around. Yet, we can easily leave the limelight to our men.

Now, what lessons have Slavic women learned that allow them to thrive in business today, while not dominating men? And what can aspiring female founders learn from them?

1. Wear different hats

A key trait is being able to switch between your personal and professional life, in order to make both successful. A Slavic woman can easily switch between her roles as a boss, a housewife, a lover and a friend. This flexibility is something that every woman should learn from a young school age as it will benefit her for the rest of her life.

2. Have a great work ethic

Don't be afraid when challenges come your way. Working for 12 hours in front of a computer is not hard; dragging train carts for 12 hours a day during the war was hard! In those days, women were the main working force and replaced men in many jobs. If we want equality, it should be everywhere; never use your gender as an excuse that you can't do something!

3. Don't compromise your femininity

While your work ethic should be on par with men, it is also key to preserve your femininity. I don't recall any period in European history since the first monarch, when Slavic women didn't wear heels. Believe me, looking and behaving like a man doesn't make men trust us more.

4. Maintain high confidence in yourself

Confidence is what makes others trust us, cooperate with us, or even invest in us. But mind you, being powerful and self-confident doesn't mean that you have to be aggressive or combative. It's actually quite the opposite! You will feel strength showing grace and mercy. When you think highly of yourself, others will do too.

5. Be fearless

Fear of failure can be numbing, but ask yourself this: What is the worst thing that can happen if we don't get a positive answer? What is really the worst-case scenario? Typically, Slavic women file away disappointing experiences in the far corners of our minds; we forget and move on. Life does not end when you hear a "No", so be fearless at what you do and treat every rejection as a step forward.

6. Be more outspoken

Slavic women are often accused of being 'too direct'. It might be true that being 100% honest may not be the most diplomatic way of communication, but this outspokenness also makes us more intuitive, inclusive and curious – all of which are important traits for entrepreneurs.

7. Get used to uncertainty

'Uncertainty' is a popular word in Silicon Valley. In the past century, Slavic women were forced many times to leave their comfort zone and figure new things out. Dealing with these situations was tough, but they enabled us to be ready to adapt whenever it's needed. In fact, many of us would be bored if life became too predictable! Always keep evolving; it's the only way to grow.

The bottom line is: Slavic women have played real men's roles in the past, and we realized that it's not something we would want to do again. That is why it is not in our blood to compete with men, and we don't need to fight for the reins. We know what we should respect men for, and we would rather be deservedly respected in return. Therefore, men are not afraid of working hand in hand with us. Does this make Slavic women submissive losers? Numbers say the opposite. So there is definitely something to learn from them.

I hope these perspectives can help you on your startup journey!

All my best,
Renata

About the author:

Renata George is a European venture capitalist based in San Francisco. As an entrepreneur, Renata has built the first local publishing house in the Central region of the Russian Federation, which created a very successful franchise business for print magazines. After that, she started helping other entrepreneurs, and soon moved to the United States to assist Central and Eastern European tech companies with their business development in the United States and worldwide. In 2012, Renata was named as one of the 'Top Women in Venture Capital and Angel Investing' by Forbes because of her active mentor work with startups. She then co-founded a venture fund, and in 2015, she joined Life.SREDA, a growth-stage FinTech VC fund based in Singapore, as Head of their US Office. Renata is one of the co-founders of Women.VC community and co-author of the first comprehensive online course on venture capital.

Letter No. 61

Lisa Goodchild, Founder and CEO of Digiwoo

Dear Female Founder,

I am writing to share with you that I am a mother of two and that I have had my own digital businesses for the last 15 years. I was an entrepreneur from the get go, always on the hustle, even as a kid. Growing up in South East London on a council estate, this is what you did: hustle.

Whatever happened in your past will make you stronger for the future. My past provided me with the essential skills for being a true entrepreneur.

People ask me how I do it all? Well, that is a good question. Being an entrepreneur can feel like a roller coaster. Hold on tight, there are lots of ups and down! But you will blink and time will disappear. It only feels like yesterday when I was 20, starting my own digital journey.

What I want you to know is:

People are everything in your work. People buy from people they like. Be nice, support, help and nurture the people around you. It is important to build your network and meet with them on a regular basis. Stay in contact via social media and face-to-face. Surround yourself with good people, like-minded people and people you can reach out to.

Confidence is something everyone thought I had, but I was fronting it most of the time. I remember me as a kid wanting to ask my mum something. I visualised how the answer was 'no' to begin with, then I would try and psych myself up, count to 10 and then go for it. I still do this but now I breathe deeply, count to 10 and tell myself I am going to own it. Whatever you want to do, own it; and I mean *really own it.*

Opportunities are there to be taken. Grab them and fly with them. The only person who can hold you back is you. When I was younger, the key reasons I had not achieved what I wanted to was because of a lack of confidence and because I did not grab opportunities. I wish I had realised what I could have achieved, if only I had gone for it. Forget about what other people think, run with your vision. Do what you love and love what you do. Don't hold yourself back, believe in yourself and remember to be gentle with yourself.

Hustle & Hard Work is what it is all about. Yes, we hear about these entrepreneurs making millions and living the dream all the time. Let's get it right. It all boils down to working every damn hour provided to make shit happen, all of which may ultimately fail. It is worth it? Hell to the yeah! It's freedom in every sense of the word. Make sure you hustle and work hard and the benefits will shine through eventually. Hang in there when it seems like it is not going anywhere. Keep calm and let it all flow.

Love your future!

Lisa

About the author:

Lisa Goodchild is a British entrepreneur based in London. Her experience in (and passion for) all things digital is unrivalled. She is the founder and CEO of Digiwoo, an integrated communications company, where she is making waves in far-reaching arenas, from fashion and food to online advertising and non-profit. Throughout her career, Lisa has brought an x-factor of excitement to her projects, making 'it' happen for the likes of Panasonic and Ted Baker in terms of brand management. She is also an advisor to notable names such as PR guru Lynne Franks, Shaa Wasmund MBE and MOBO Awards founder Kanya King MBE. Lisa does what she loves and loves what she does – whether that's being a mother, getting creative with communications, or turning her digital passions into celebrated success stories.

Letter No. 62

Natasha Tiwari, Founder and CEO of The Tutoring Team (T3) and Xarii.com

Dear Female Founder,

Humans were made to create. We all have something special about us, and creating things is how we put that out into the world. For all of the budding entrepreneurs out there, this is the beginning of a truly heroic, creative journey, where you will take risks, discover new things, and experience the highest of highs. And, along the way, you will become transformed. Congratulations, you. I decided at a young age that I would like to work for myself, but never would have guessed that it would have been so soon in my career, nor predicted the insane journey it would have been to date. Comparing my younger self to now, my ideas have continually developed, my dreams are coming alive, and my visions for the future are soaring.

Fresh out of my postgraduate university studies, aged 22, I founded an education company called The Tutoring Team (T3), aiming to change the tutoring world, disrupting the way how private supplementary education happens, and challenging traditional learning concepts across the world, whilst raising expectations for children we work with. People always ask how I got started, at a relatively young age. After having worked for other people, always feeling frustrated when I felt things could be done better or feeling bored when the pace was too slow for me, I couldn't bear to work like that again. Upon founding T3, I didn't call myself an entrepreneur. In my mind, I was just a girl, who was excited about creating something new, in the name of being rebellious and avoiding a 'proper job' - ha! Even now, five years on, with two growing ventures, I think of myself that way, and am hoping I'll never lose that attitude I started out with.

Succeeding in your entrepreneurial journey will involve a combination of fantastic ideas and excellent execution. Whilst it is wise to be practical and pragmatic in your work (there is always tonnes to do), I believe that it is important to strive for excellence when building your products and constructing your services. Hold yourself to the highest of standards – this approach will pay off. A product or service, which is truly enchanting, will be the foundation of why your customers love you and why your business grows. At T3, we are a relatively small and young firm compared to others in the industry, but I have found that we have been successful in forging exciting partnerships and securing some amazing accounts, with some of the world's most influential people, because the services we provide are unique, and we are able to boast an incredible track record of results because of it. Our growth and impact is fundamentally fuelled by the effort that goes into making sure our services are truly fantastic.

A lot of talk happens in startup circles about 'Minimum Viable Products'; but in my opinion, creating a *loveable* product is more important. The aesthetics (depending on your business, of course) and the superficial details don't need to be perfect, but the crux of the product/service should be stellar for you to compete in your space and make maximum impact for your clients and customers. If building a company is like building your own utopia, then excellence should sit at the centre of your universe. Whenever I have hit my milestones for the impact we wish to make as a company, but also personally in my work, I get this buzzing feeling. It is the best feeling in the world. But you can only know that you have hit those highs, when you have carefully set your targets before and have relevant KPIs in place. Only that which gets measured, can be improved, and duly celebrated.

Entrepreneurs are often the most self-critical and it is easy to fall into the trap of feeling like your progress or performance hasn't been enough, if you don't have benchmarks to measure yourself against. I have certainly been guilty of this, so my advice is to set a few key metrics and be clear on how they relate to your goals as well as how they fit with the stage in which your business is in. Taking this approach has allowed me to measure and assess our own growth, set targets for the future, and most importantly, know whether we are on the right track. It is so easy to ruminate on things that don't go to plan and to skim over things that do. Make sure to celebrate your wins! The big ones are your milestones, the little ones are the stepping stones taking you there. Both are fundamental. And when you don't achieve your goals, remember that every successful person has failed before. Perfection is a myth, as is success without effort.

All successful entrepreneurs I know work harder than anyone else, and it should be said that that is a good thing. Nobody ever built anything incredible on a 9-5 schedule, but grant yourself time to reflect and recuperate when you need to. I find that the real magical moments of inspiration come to me in those moments when I take pause. Any innovator knows: inspiration is the lifeline of creativity. When you feel low or depleted, remind yourself why you are doing it all, and you will put yourself back on the right path. I find it's easy to become obsessed and workaholic, but keep a life outside of work too. Keep your social life in tact and keep doing the things you enjoy doing. You serve your business best when you are the happiest and most balanced version of yourself. Surround yourself with people who are on the same path as you, but also keep your friends and family as a part of your journey – no one will ever be as proud of you as they will. In good times, they will be the first to celebrate. In tougher times, they will be your pillars of support and most likely will surprise you with how well they know you. If you have made a commitment to uproot your life and become an entrepreneur, you are here to change the world; but your world is nothing without the people who you love and cherish.

Last year, hungry for a new challenge, I started Xarii.com with a mission to change the way people shop for Indian fashion online. At Xarii, we are still very much in our infancy, but we are making waves, working with exciting designers, and selling the most beautiful clothes. This is my first foray into tech entrepreneurship and fashion. An eCommerce venture has been a wholly different animal to building a consultancy, but I have seen how the lessons I have learnt along the way translate between the two companies. One core learning has been striking a balance between that which is fun, and that which is necessary; whilst creativity and passion keeps your business innovative and competitive, it is logistics and the ability to build systems, which will allow you to scale quickly.

Keep your mind open to the lessons that can be learned, even when it is not totally obvious. Launching Xarii.com, with no background in fashion or technology, gave me a sense that anything is possible if you put your mind to it. Undoubtedly, I had to go through a tougher and far steeper learning curve than if I would have had a fashion tech background, but I have made a conscious effort to really enjoy every part of the journey, particularly when I have been most challenged. So when things feel heavy, remind yourself to have a good time. Entrepreneurship should be a fun endeavour!

If you take anything away from my letter, please take this: No matter your age, gender or knowledge, if you have passion, a solid work ethic, and an incredible idea, you have an exciting path ahead as an entrepreneur. Be curious, be tenacious, and don't ever stop making your own luck. I'll leave you with words from my favourite poet, Rumi: "Live life like everything is rigged in your favour."

With love,
Natasha

About the author:

Natasha Tiwari is a British-Indian serial entrepreneur based in London. She is the founder of The Tutoring Team (T3), a global education advisory and tutoring company based in London, where she and her team of 70 accelerate the rates at which students learn, to achieve academic goals, using innovative, unique methods; counting royal families and celebrities amongst their clients. She also works with a research-based organisation out of Stanford University on the topics of positive behavioural change and lectures internationally on building optimum mindsets for learning, heroism in children and emotional intelligence. In 2015, Natasha's creative instincts led her to founding her second venture, a fashion e-commerce startup, Xarii.com, selling affordable luxury Indian and Indian inspired fashion online. Natasha is a two time graduate of University College London and has an academic background in psychology and politics.

Letter No. 63

Sarah Kunst, Founder and CEO of Proday

Dear Female Founder,

It's always nice to meet a kindred spirit on this journey, because it's so damn lonely. The long nights, constant to-do lists, unrelenting stress and slow acceptance that every action causes an equal and opposite deluge of work are kind of terrifying. I often joke that starting a company must be like having a kid – if you had any clue how hard it was, you'd never do it.

But here I am, rocking my startup baby at 5:22am, making sure to attend to its every hiccup and fuss, while dreaming of the bright beautiful future that lies ahead. I imagine how proud I'll be when I raise that round or hit profitability. I hum a lullaby of growth.

The constant responsibility floors you at first. Realizing that you are the one responsible for payroll, product vision, buying the toilet paper, and that whatever you aren't doing in a given moment often isn't getting done. Your unsigned contract or too slow sales cycle or missed investor email might mean the difference between success and failure. It's humbling. And maddening. But ultimately empowering.

See, most of us grow up as overachievers, really great at the things we do. We casually ace tests, circumnavigate the globe and get into the college of our dreams. We follow directions, get extra credit and tick off so many boxes. The boxes! If boxes were Teslas, we would all drive.

But at some point we have earned every accolade and achievement. We start to suspect that we could do it better on our own. The call to entrepreneurship comes early for some and accidentally for others. Like an alarm, it pierces our consciousness and cannot be unheard. We become woke. And that's when the adventure begins.

We study how to run a company the same way we prepared for exams, but at the end of the reading there's no essay or multiple-choice test, instead we just start. It doesn't take long to learn that we aren't nearly as good as we thought we were, but we get better daily.

Incorporating a company while launching an app while negotiating with investors while onboarding a hire? Sure, I'll have it done by noon. Then I'll turn to the spreadsheets and emails, and wonder how high an inbox count goes before I trigger a personal Y2K.

We leave high-powered jobs to become our own assistants and interns. We learn that we can in fact fail 100 times before breakfast and then forget it all when a huge victory comes in before lunch. We kiss goodbye the long weekend brunches and summer Fridays. We embrace the constant flow of more work. In exchange we become CEOs and Board Presidents. If we're lucky and the creek don't rise, we emerge from a decade long chrysalis of non-stop work as a success, replete with the attendant money and power.

We always have a seat at the table, because we built it from scratch after a late night run to IKEA. We have opportunities and authority that women before us could not have dreamed of. We pave a path for the girls behind us and are a beacon for those among us. We survive the gauntlet and we finally get some sleep.

Sweet dreams,
Sarah

About the author:

Sarah Kunst is an American entrepreneur based between New York and San Francisco. She is the founder and CEO of Proday, a personal training fitness app that allows you to workout alongside professional athletes. Besides running her own venture, she also mentors and advises startups through Boost.vc, MergeLane, and Female Funders. Sarah is on the 2015 Forbes Magazine 30 under 30 list and named a top 25 innovator in tech by Cool Hunting. Her philanthropic interests include Venture for America, Code2040, and The US State Department's Tech Women program. She is a contributing editor at Marie Claire Magazine and also writes for TechCrunch, The Daily Beast and Entrepreneur.com. Marc Andreessen named her one of his 55 Unknown Rock Stars in Tech.

Letter No. 64

Chanyu Xu, Co-Founder of Eating.de

Dear Female Founder,

I was 22 years old and in the middle of my university degree when I decided to start my first company. I had no clue about the concept of "software as a service", let alone how to build an Internet company. My family and friends were very shocked when they learnt about my decision.

To understand this reaction, I have to tell you a bit more about my family background:

My dad left China in 1986 and came to West Germany with two suitcases and $500. Back then it was not easy for a Chinese person to get an immigration visa, but my family had the right connections ("guanxi" as the Chinese would say), and my dad got out.

He left his pregnant wife (my mom) and his unborn child (me) in China to start a new life on the other side of the world. His German skills were no more than "Guten Tag" (hello), "Bitte" (please) and "Danke" (thank you). He studied at a German university, but $500 were gone fast, so he started working at Chinese restaurants to support himself. And soon enough, he chose to drop out of university to start his own business.

My mom joined him in Germany one year after I was born, leaving me with my grandparents in China (a common thing to do in Asia).

Together, they lived on a very low budget, so that after three years, they had enough savings to start a limited company to open their first restaurant. That was the time, when I joined them in Germany and our family was finally reunited.

My parents always supported the family with their own business and never received any financial aid from the German government. Through their hard work, they were able to provide a great life for my younger brother and me. We had every opportunity and chance to advance in society – all doors were wide open.

But here is the difference: my parents became entrepreneurs out of necessity, I became one out of choice. In their minds, their hard work should result in my university education, which would enable me to get a well-paid, stable job at a big corporation. My dad was furious when I told him that I wasn't going to join a corporate after graduation. He thought I was crazy for putting my education at risk and starting an Internet company instead.

I couldn't blame him. It was 2009 and Germany was in the midst of the financial crisis – probably not the best time to start an Internet company. I still did. The first year as a rookie entrepreneur was tough. We had no funding and bootstrapped everything. When we got €60,000 from our first business angels, it felt like we could conquer the world. In the first draft of our business plan, we seriously thought that we would break-even with a €200,000 investment! That is when I learnt my first business lesson.

You always need more money than you think. Once you start scaling the business, you will not only need to hire more people, but also pay yourself a small salary. A founder who is struggling with her personal finances can't focus on the business. Make sure your investors understand that too.

In 2013, I decided to leave my first company to follow my passion and start a new business in the online food delivery sector. I guess the apple doesn't fall far from the tree. After accepting my first bold career decision and acknowledging our achievements in scaling the business to nearly 60 employees, my dad was deeply shocked (again) when I told him that I changed my mind. But it was not the decision itself that upset him, it was the fact that I wanted to do something in the food sector – he knew how hard it was.

Listen to your gut. It's hard to explain why I left my first company after being through a rollercoaster ride for 3.5 years. It was my personal (maybe selfish) decision, but my gut told me it was the right thing to do. When it's time to move on, move on!

I started a healthy food delivery service in Berlin. Thousands of people were using food ordering platforms on a daily basis, but back then you could mainly order pizza, sushi or Asian food. There were no healthy, non-fast food options. I created the recipes that we produced, managed a kitchen, 20 drivers and daily operations as a single founder. Business was growing and soon we opened a second branch in another part of the city, but I just couldn't handle it on my own anymore. I hardly slept and had almost no social interactions with friends or family.

Always get a co-founder. If I had do everything again, that's probably the only little thing I would do differently: I would avoid starting a company without a co-founder. Having someone who shares the same vision, works alongside you, and sticks with you through the bad times is just priceless. I reached a point where the pressure of my startup was bringing me down, so I had two options: I could stop and fail, or continue and destroy myself. I chose the first option.

Sometimes you win, sometimes you learn. Admitting and accepting to fail let's you grow massively on a personal level. Take your time to reflect all experiences, the good, the bad and the ugly. Don't feel ashamed to fail. The important thing is how you do it. Be honest and communicate openly with employees, shareholders, investors and business partners why things did not work out.

In 2014, I had my personal David vs. Goliath moment. I had the option between a small team with an idea that triggered my passion or the opportunity to build a startup with a big corporation (some call it the dark side). I chose the dark side.

After 5 years and the recent experience as a single founder, I needed a (mental) break from grassroots entrepreneurship. I was always curious about how to scale a business fast and with seemingly 'endless' options, so I became country co-founder for a food delivery venture backed with lots of money. If it wasn't for this specific opportunity, I wouldn't have joined the big ship, but I was able to work with some of the brightest talents I have ever met and it proved to be a great experience. However, the adrenalin junkie in me wanted more.

Life is too short to not pursue your dreams. The idea from 2014 was still stuck in my head and I decided to leave the big ship. In the summer of 2015, I founded eating.de together with Clemens and Jochen, whom I met through mutual friends and who both had an entrepreneurial background. I combined all learnings from past (ad)ventures, and started working on something that truly makes me happy together with co-founders who have complementary skills to me.

No matter what you do, you will always come across people who think your idea is nuts and who will call you crazy. Ignore those people and just keep going. I am passionate about eating.de, because I believe that a clean and well-balanced diet is the foundation of a healthy, long life. That is why I want to give people a healthy, tasty and convenient food option every day – to improve their lives. It might sound nuts, but to me, there is nothing else I would rather do in this world!

It's okay to have a private life. Let's not fool ourselves – building a company is really exhausting, both mentally and physically. Make sure you eat, sleep and exercise enough. It's okay to take some time off and enjoy yourself with non-work related stuff. The external pressure is already high enough, so please don't put additional pressure on yourself. I, for instance, started to meditate and found that it helped me to focus and prioritise better.

Remember there is no right or wrong. Just do what you want or need to do. I never wanted to be a 'one day' person and I'm aware that I had the incredible, ultimate privilege of freedom of choice, thanks to my parents' hard work. Even if you are not that lucky, do something that makes you happy. This way, you won't look back 'one day' and think 'what if'.

I'm sure there are plenty of things that I still need to learn on my journey, but for the time being I enjoy every blood, sweat and tear drop that comes with it to the fullest.

Why don't you join me? It is the most rewarding thing you can do.

Best,
Chanyu

About the author:

Chanyu Xu is a Chinese-born serial entrepreneur and foodie based in Berlin. She is currently the co-founder of Eating.de, an online food production company that offers pre-cooked functional dishes and fine dining menus as a subscription service. The company has received a 7-digit amount seed investment from Holtzbrinck Ventures and Peter Thiel's Founders Fund. Prior to founding Eating.de, Chanyu run two other startups (one very successful, the other one a bit less). She was also the country co-founder of EatFirst in Germany, backed by Rocket Internet. She holds a master's degree in Strategic Communications from Berlin University of the Arts and is a big supporter of women in tech and entrepreneurship.

Letter No. 65

Kristina Naruseviciute, Co-Founder of Smartup Visuals

Dear Female Founder,

I dare to compare entrepreneurship to surfing, and that is why I created this visual metaphor to share with you. Metaphors are one of the fundamental teaching tools to help people learn, and I think if you have ever attempted to surf, body board, or even swim in the ocean, then you will relate to this metaphor.

And if you haven't, then perhaps you will find yourself wondering: do I want to be a watcher on the shore? Or maybe it is time to try to catch 'my wave'?

I wish I could have shared these ideas with a younger version of myself – knowing what I know now about entrepreneurship and its difficulties would have made navigating the ocean of complexity much, much easier. I started as a freelance designer and ended up building a visual communication agency. Practicing and delivering a design service is one thing, creating an organisation and running a business is another. It requires your constant attention and is a permanent balancing act. Entrepreneurship is a way of life. It is a mindset.

A surfer girl would never throw herself out into unknown. She learns what to do before she hits the ocean. Equally, it's really helpful for you to understand how things work from people who have tried before. Use all the resources you can access. If you can afford a private lesson, then hire a business mentor.

Once you have learned and prepared as much as you can, there is nothing else you can do, except for trying it yourself. Try to balance your own board, get smashed by the big waves and pounding surf, and eventually figure out the thrill of getting the timing right, building that momentum and riding that wave. Hooray, you have made it!

Enjoy the surf,
Kristina

About the author:

Kristina Naruseviciute is a Lithuanian entrepreneur based in London. She is the co-founder of Smartup Visuals, a visual communication agency. Her team is made up of artists, designers, illustrators and animators that specialise in helping companies, particularly startups, communicate their business effectively and creatively. She and her team have supported large organisations and global events, such as the BBC, Tech City UK, Level 39, Barclay's Rise, LinkedIn, and TEDx, as well as startups like Grabble, Splittable, and Geek Girl Meetup in London. Kristina works across geographies and cultures utilising art as an ideation and communication tool to help bridge the various barriers that exist within organisations. Her background is in fine arts with a focus on creative thinking, design and innovation. She studied at Central Saint Martins and won 1st place in a competition for young artists in Lithuania.

ENTREPRENEURSHIP IS SURFING

1. Learn to read the ocean. It's much more than what you see from the shore. Understand your market.

2. To catch a wave, first you have to paddle through them. You might need to hustle before people buy what you're selling.

3. You'll get some salty water up you nose. It won't feel pleasant! Learn from the critique.

4. Be Patient. Your wave will take time. Building a business can be a time consuming process. It won't happen overnight!

5. You'll fall, over and over again... get up and keep doing what you came here to do!

6. Other surfers can teach and inspire you, but you will have to do the hard work yourself. Learn from your competitors and other entrepreneurs.

7. Challenges are opportunities. Bad weather may mean stronger, better waves. There are no problems, only opportunities in disguise.

9. There is always another wave.

8. Once you're up, enjoy the ride! Stay present and don't forget to balance.

10. We can't control the ocean but we can learn how to ride the waves.

SMARTUP VISUALS

Letter No. 66

Toni Lane Casserly, Co-Founder of CoinTelegraph and Kids Compassion Charity

Dear Female Founder,

I am going to start by telling you a story – one I don't necessarily want to share, but one I will willingly grant to the commons with the hopes that each and every one of you will be able to grow from understanding my experience.

I was getting married once. I never did.

I never associated the idea of marriage with my identity, my self-worth, or ownership. When I made the decision to give my life to another being, it was because I authentically fell in love with an equal who wholeheartedly loved me back. We wrote a 200-page book together. Each line was overflowing with poetry and emotional candor from the deep and meaningful love letters we had penned during our intervals apart. We travelled the world together, one that he had never seen. He made me laugh, and when I needed a soldier, he fought for me. I had never experienced that before. A person who loved me unconditionally.

Everything was... perfect. A blissful bubble of peace and harmony with all of the respect and equanimity I needed to courageously embark on the journey to share the rest of my life with one person; we were as empowered and sovereign as ever.

I was ready. I was happy. I was free.

I was, until my private life and media empire fell under savage assault from a group of women who felt threatened by my presence and my success.

The destructive and scorned women saw themselves as 'competitors' in red oceans instead of collaborators in the blue. With smiling faces, they portrayed their character as that of cordial angels, but in reality, their toxic and fragile hands clasped broken glass. They tried to annihilate me in the most effective way they knew how to – by causing me personal pain.

From day one, this group of female bloggers had received my professional and personal support in a myriad of ways. I had my media company write articles promoting them, I connected them with invaluable resources for their careers, I stood by them during illnesses, and tried to provide them with courage to keep their thoughts positive in times of stress and healing. I had been kind to them (looking back, far too kind), which is why the last thing I expected was for these women to form a 'circle of hate' around me, attempting to mutilate my life and my work.

With social manipulation and reckless cruelty, these women, who largely consider each other to be enemies, banded together in hate to create a series of fabricated lies engineered to hurt the one thing I loved more than language – my life partner. Contacting my other half, they poisoned his mind with violent, cruel and hateful rumors. Lies that eventually led to forms of social abuse as mild as group isolation, as severe as death threats. For the first time in my life, I felt fragile, weak, without recourse or a shred of hope.

I was broken. Broken, but not defeated.

The man I loved, however, was a different story.

After a person whose word he possessed a great deal of credence for, a person he was indebted to, began to play game with my attackers, he could not bear the weight brought on by the fear of future grief, and when the trust was completely eliminated, we broke.

Alone, but alive with dignity, I had nothing but my company and the dreams of a future that could be.

I look back at this now, and I am overwhelmed. Truly possessed by an immense feeling of... hate, despair, loss? No. I am profoundly overwhelmed with the feeling of gratitude.

And I laugh about this experience, my God, do I laugh. Why? Because truly, it is funny. How daunting this seemed at first. How unjust this punishment for bravery.

I was at a loss, but I had won.

If there is one thing I have learned about the road of life, it is that your path is largely determined by your state of mind and of course, your friends, the people who truly love you unconditionally. Perceptions and emotions are as much of a choice as your actions, so take care to remember, unexpected trials can and should lead towards greater unexpected bliss. Your thoughts become things. Manifest destiny and remember that the moment you come to think you have everything figured out, this world will show you know nothing at all.

The only truth you can ever hope to know is that you will always be learning.

Yes, I do. I do, under any circumstances, accept the past with grace, because I know how lucky I am to have had these experiences. At the end of the day, I have been provided with the greatest gift: a story to share with you and a smarter, stronger, more evolved self.

So I ask you, who are you? You are not a color, a name, an object, or a gender. You are the fearless ambition of freedom embodied. Every breath you take, whether through struggle or success, is a step towards greater being. You have the power to take your life into your own hands and make a more extraordinary future. Rise above it all and soar to the sky. Heaven is your potential, every dream is within your grasp!

If hate attempts to hold you down, defy it. Defy hate with the mind of a warrior and the heart of a saint, because hate is a human at war with themselves. Do not let their battles slow you down or become your own. There are bigger, more important wars to be won. You have a world to take on, so let your powerful empathy be a gift, not a setback.

As for my story, the man I wrote about is now with the love of his life and I have to say, I am incomprehensibly happy for them.

After all of this, how do I feel?

I feel so ready. I feel so happy. I feel so free.

Cliché as it may be, I still hold the belief that through all of the empire building, the great fun and the extraordinary journey, I will find the most pure and remarkable love this world has to offer. The love that is right for me.

Women, love yourself first. Honor yourself with the same strength and compassion you use to honor others. Financial freedom is the only freedom. You can depend on yourself. You are secure. If you want to see a cultural shift in this world, embody it.

So, who are you to me? You are a hero, a best friend, a sister, a mother, a daughter, a revolutionary.

You are not a product, you make them.

Go forth and fight for the change you want to see in this world.

With love, respect and admiration,
-Toni Lane Casserly, TLC

About the author:

Toni Lane Casserly is an American tech entrepreneur, artist and thought leader based on planet Earth. She is a Young Star of Bitcoin and the co-founder of CoinTelegraph, the largest media network in the bitcoin and blockchain industries. As a philanthropist, Toni Lane co-founded Kids Compassion Charity when she funded a village to survive Ebola using bitcoin. As part of this endeavor, she put 14 children through school and has provided 14 orphans with a home. Toni Lane currently works toward establishing digital currency economies, mesh internets and peaceful seasteads to help free citizens from the hands of war-torn, oppressive and corrupt leadership while preserving the planet. In addition to her work as a technology entrepreneur, she is also the founder of the 'post art' movement, also known as 'immaterialism', a new form of art, which uses consciousness as a medium.

ACKNOWLEDGMENTS

"We cannot build our own future without helping other to build theirs."

– Bill Clinton

This book would not exist without the incredible women who took time out of their (very) busy schedules to sit down and write their letters to you. I was overwhelmed by their positive response and truly grateful for their willingness to help. Writing these letters is not an easy task and is certainly not something that can be done on a whim. Therefore, I cannot thank every single one of them enough for their support.

Additionally, I owe special thanks:

To David Brown, for kindly contributing the Foreword and supporting the cause.

To Mike Butcher, who graciously shared my project on social media, allowing me to connect with some amazing contributors.

To Chantal Marin, who reached out on my behalf and connected me with over 20 interested women, while working on two startups and studying for her Masters degree.

To Nancy Fechnay, for being super supportive and connecting me with various contributors as well as endorsers.

To Irra Ariella Khi, for believing in me and championing the book from the moment we spoke on the phone (she didn't know me and was waiting at an Austrian airport for her luggage at the time).

To Shefaly Yogendra, for guiding me through things a newbie author/editor wouldn't find intuitive; for example, the difference between a copyright release form, a copyright transfer agreement and a copyright license agreement.

To Belinda Budge and Andrew Cunning, for giving precious feedback.

To Lucy Fernandez Lau, for spending her Friday nights helping me to design the book cover.

To my Startup Weekend & Techstars community family, through whom I have learnt about the importance of community in the startup world. I'm so glad I met you!

To the amazing women in the Blooming Founders community who give me a reason to get up in the morning and work on something meaningful. Keep blooming, ladies!

To my proofreading team: Azra Ali, Isabelle Brennan, Katherine Church, Emma Sheppard and Cathy Ayre who helped prevent a non-native speaker from embarrassing herself. Thank you for donating your time and brainpower. I am taking responsibility for all remaining typos or grammar mistakes that survived our rigorous screening process (I hope, it's not too bad).

To Crystal Brent, Priya Sapre and Diane Chaleff, who helped me edit some tough parts.

To every person who has supported me along the way, either by making introductions or by generously offering feedback. You know who you are!

Finally, a big thank you to my mother, for not pressuring me to adhere to societal standards and letting me pursue my entrepreneurial dreams, even though I don't tell her a lot about what I am doing (it's for your own peace of mind, mum!). And to my late father, who got us to Germany and provided us with access to a life with limitless opportunities.

And last but not least, a heartfelt thank you to you, dear reader, for reading this far!

You might not be a founder, or female, but I am grateful that you were interested in the content and I hope that you got inspired and have learned a thing or two about how to deal with the challenges of entrepreneurship, especially for women. If you did, please share with others, whether they are women or men, young or old, working in a startup or corporate organisation.

And if you are a female founder, then I would love to welcome you to the Blooming Founders community. See you there!

London
May 2016

ABOUT THE EDITOR

Lu Li is a serial entrepreneur, creative innovator and pragmatic optimist. She is currently obsessed about inspiring, educating and championing other women to build sustainable businesses in order to achieve freedom and fulfillment in their professional lives.

Her own entrepreneurial journey has involved an image consulting service as well as a consulting firm in the tourism industry. In her third business, Blooming Founders, she is now focusing on creating new solutions that lead aspiring and budding female entrepreneurs to find business success faster.

Lu has been invited to mentor at the Google Launchpad accelerator programme and is also one of the Techstars community leaders. Additionally, she has been appointed the UK ambassador for Women's Entrepreneurship Day, which is celebrated annually at the United Nations and around the globe.

She speaks regularly at conferences about the challenges of female entrepreneurship and how to overcome them. She is also frequently invited to inspire university students on entrepreneurship and has delivered talks for the London School of Economics, London Business School, Cass Business School, University College London (UCL) and HULT International Business School.

Before Lu discovered the opportunities and freedom of entrepreneurship, she was a diligent corporate soldier, working for the likes of McKinsey & Company and Procter & Gamble.

Occasionally, she is known as a language geek who is fluent in three languages (German, Mandarin Chinese, English). She also has studied Latin and Ancient Greek for 7 and 5 years, respectively, and is looking forward to master more languages in her lifetime.

When she is not working on building her business, Lu can be found trying new restaurants for brunch, travelling somewhere to spend quality time with her friends, and indulging in a matcha latte or karaoke (sometimes even at the same time).

She can be reached on lu.li@bloomingfounders.com or @houseofli on Twitter.

ABOUT BLOOMING FOUNDERS

Blooming Founders is an organisation, which exists to reinvent the experience of startup incubation for women, addressing unique struggles that female founders face, whilst helping entrepreneurs of both genders succeed in their journey.

We do this by providing a community of peer support for enterprising women and useful content for both male and female founders in form of events, a newsletter, blog and now this book.

Our products are designed for women, because we found that existing support in the startup ecosystem didn't do a good enough job to cater to female interests and needs. We really want to see more women-led businesses succeed and therefore took on the challenge of creating an innovative support structure that helps female founders effectively.

This doesn't mean that we are anti-men. In fact, we firmly believe that entrepreneurship is a level playing field that should be inclusive to everyone, whilst allowing for protective spaces where sub-communities with a similar mindset or identity can support and push each other forward.

If you would like to work with us or support us, feel free to connect via hello@bloomingfounders.com or @bloomingfoundrs on Twitter.

To follow our progress, please sign up to our newsletter at www.bloomingfounders.com/newsletter.

There are lots of ideas in the pipeline and we are very excited to bring them to life.

Made in the USA
Coppell, TX
18 September 2020

38302623R00184